I0459601

LIFE SKILLS FOR TEENS AND YOUNG ADULTS

THE ULTIMATE STEP-BY-STEP GUIDE TO BUILD INDEPENDENCE, ACHIEVE CONFIDENCE, AND MASTER REAL-WORLD SKILLS TO THRIVE IN JUST 30 DAYS

ALEXANDER KNIGHT

GK CREATIVE ENTERPRISES, LLC

INTRODUCTION

Looking back on when I was a teen, I can vividly remember the day I got my first paycheck from a summer job. I was so thrilled that I went straight down to the mall, spending it all on clothes and gadgets. A short time after this, I soon realized I had nothing left for savings or even for the bus fare to get to work the next week – I'd blown it all. This experience taught me an important lesson when it comes to handling money—one that I had to learn the hard way.

This book is designed to help you navigate similar challenges. The goal is simple: to provide a practical, step-by-step guide to mastering life skills that will make you more confident and independent. Now here's for the incredible part: we're going to do all this in just 30 days.

Life skills are crucial for everyone, but they are often overlooked in traditional education. Did you know that 93% of employers nowadays consider soft skills like communication and teamwork to be equally or more important than technical skills? Yet, these are rarely taught in schools. Take for example a study by the Pew Research Center, which found that 61% of young adults feel unprepared for the real world. This book aims to bridge that gap by equipping you with the skills you need to thrive.

This book is ideally suited to teens and young adults who are eager to take control of their lives. It's also for parents though, who want to support their children in becoming responsible, capable adults. If you fall into one of these categories, you're bound to find valuable insights and practical advice here – so, keeping reading on.

The structure of this book is straightforward. Each chapter focuses on a specific life skill:

- **Financial Literacy:** Learn how to budget, save, and invest your money wisely.
- **Cooking:** Basic recipes and kitchen skills that everyone should know.
- **Time Management:** Tips for organizing your day and prioritizing tasks.
- **Personal Hygiene:** Essential habits for maintaining cleanliness and health.
- **First Aid:** Basic medical knowledge that can make a big difference in emergencies.
- **Mental Health:** Strategies for managing stress and maintaining emotional well-being.
- **Social Skills:** How to build strong relationships and communicate effectively.
- **Career Readiness:** Tips for job hunting, resume writing, and interview preparation.

- **Home Maintenance:** Basic skills for taking care of your living space.
- **Digital Literacy:** Understanding technology and using it responsibly.
- **Building Independence:** Steps to becoming more self-reliant.
- **Personal Growth:** Setting goals and working towards them.

By the end of this 30-day program, you'll feel more confident, independent, but also be prepared to face real-world challenges. You'll know how to handle your finances, cook a decent meal, manage your time, and much more. The hope is that these transformations will not only make your life easier, but also more fulfilling – opening up a wide variety of opportunities that you'd previously thought impossible.

But before we get into, let me introduce myself: I'm Alexander Knight. What do I bring to the table, you ask? Well, for starters, a strong background in Developmental Psychology. I've spent years mentoring young people and helping them navigate the complexities of social dynamics. This all stems from my belief in the transformative power of nurtured social connections and the advancement in personal growth. Seeing firsthand how practical skills can empower teens to achieve their full potential, has kept me motivated to assist others on their journeys towards fulfillment.

Just another quick note before we being - this book is not just a collection of tips and advice. It's rather a call to action. I encourage you to engage actively with the content, complete the exercises and apply the lessons you'll learn to your daily lives. After all, consistency and effort are key to achieving the transformation you seek. So, as you pop your shoes on and walk with me on this journey, remember that every day presents a new opportunity to learn and grow. You have the power to shape your future, and this book is here to guide you every step of the way. Who's ready to dive in?

CHAPTER ONE

MASTERING FINANCIAL LITERACY

A t a young age, many people experience the excitement of getting their first paycheck, only to quickly become puzzled by how fast their money disappears. Such experiences often highlight the need for a better understanding of how to manage finances effectively. After all said and done, financial literacy isn't just about saving money; it's about making informed decisions that will offer a sense of security and form a stepping-stone to allow you to have so many more adventures.

1.1 CREATING A PERSONAL BUDGET

Understanding your in-goings and out-goings is the foundation of financial health – so, let's zero in on this before anything else. Essentially, it's like having a map that shows you where you are and where you need to go. Income can come from various sources—allowances, part-time jobs, or even gifts from relatives. Each type of income needs to be tracked so you know exactly how much money you have. Think of your expenses as two squads: Team Fixed and Team Variable. Team Fixed is super consistent – always showing up with the same energy each month, like your phone bill or those must-have subscription services. Team Variable, on the other hand, likes to mix it up. One month, it's splurging on a new outfit; the next it's movie nights or school supplies – always keeping things interesting!

Let's look at this practically; you might spend $20 on a new book this month but nothing the next. That's a variable expense. But don't fear, tracking these expenses can be easy with the right tools. Apps like You Need a Budget (YNAB) or spreadsheets can help you keep track of everything and in one place. Plus, you can categorize everything!

Setting financial goals is crucial. It gives your budgeting efforts a purpose and helps you stay motivated. Let's think about it – short term goals might be saving up for a concert ticket or a new video game. These are goals you can achieve in a few weeks or months. Long-term goals, however, require more planning and patience, like saving for college or buying a car. To set effective goals, use the SMART framework.

Specific: Clearly define the goal you want to achieve. Make it precise and detailed. For example, instead of saying "I want to save money," specify "I want to save $200 for a new bike."

Measurable: Establish criteria to track your progress. Ensure you can measure how much you have achieved and assess whether you are on track. For instance, you can measure progress by how much you save each week or month.

Achievable: Set a realistic goal that you can accomplish with the resources and time available. It should be challenging but attainable. For example, saving $200 in three months should be achievable if you budget accordingly.

Relevant: Ensure the goal is meaningful and aligned with your broader objectives. It should be relevant to your needs or aspirations. Saving money for a new bike should be relevant if it supports your personal or recreational goals.

Time-bound: Set a clear deadline for when you want to achieve the goal. This helps create urgency and keeps you motivated. For example, aim to save $200 within three months.

This clarity helps you stay focused and track your progress. We'll come back to SMART goals throughout this book, as they can prove effective in many situations.

Creating a budget plan tailored to your lifestyle involves several steps. (1) Start by listing all your sources of income and then categorize your expenses. Allocate funds to different categories like needs, wants, and savings. A common method is the 50/30/20 rule, where 50% of your income goes to needs, 30% to wants, and 20% to savings. This rule helps you balance essential expenses with fun activities and saving for the future. (2) Adjust your budget as your income or expenses change. If you get a raise at work, you might want to save more or allocate extra funds to a specific goal.

This monitoring and adjusting of your budget is just as important as creating it in the first place. Remember: a budget is not set in stone; it should evolve with your financial situation.

Conduct Monthly Budget Reviews: Regularly assess your budget to track your adherence to the plan.

Identify Overspending: Look for areas where you may be spending more than planned and pinpoint specific categories of excess.

Develop Cutting Strategies: Create plans to reduce unnecessary expenses based on your findings.

Example of Adjustment: If excessive spending on takeout is identified, consider cooking more meals at home to save money.

Stay on Track: Use these reviews to make informed decisions and ensure your spending habits align with your financial goals.

Developing a personal budget might seem daunting at first, but it's a necessary skill that will serve you well throughout your life. Understanding where your money comes from and where it goes gives you control over your financial future. With a clear budget, you can set and achieve your financial goals, making it easier to face real-world challenges. How about pausing now, opening up a new spreadsheet and beginning to get a grasp on your finances?

1.2 UNDERSTANDING BANK ACCOUNTS AND SAVINGS

Navigating the many different varieties of bank accounts available can seem stressful, but understanding these can make managing your money go much more smoothly.

A checking account is where most people start. It's ideal for everyday transactions like buying lunch or paying for school supplies. You'll get a debit card to make these purchases, and you can also write checks if needed. Checking accounts often come with online banking options, making it easy to monitor your balance and transactions.

Savings accounts, on the other hand, are designed to help you save money over time. They usually offer higher interest rates compared to checking accounts, meaning your money can grow while it sits there. These accounts are great for setting aside funds for larger goals, like a fun trip with friends. They are there to encourage saving, so frequent withdrawals might come with fees, so always read the terms and conditions when you sign up.

Apart from those first two options, joint accounts with parents can be a useful option for teens. These accounts allow for both parent and child to monitor and manage the funds, providing a safety net while coming of age, learning the ropes of financial independence.

Opening a bank account is fairly straightforward. Really, you just need to gather the required identification and some other documents. You'll usually need a government-issued ID, like a driver's license or passport, and your Social Security number. Some banks might also require proof of address, such as a utility bill. You can choose between online and in-person banking options depending on your preference.

Online banking is convenient and allows you to manage your account from anywhere. At the same time, visiting a branch in-person can provide a clearer understanding of the services offered and give you a chance to ask questions if you have any doubts. Although nowadays, there's also a wealth of info online you can access in just a few clicks.

Once your account is open, it's good practice to keep track of your statements. Regularly reviewing these helps you monitor your spending and catch any potential unauthorized transactions, though these are rare. Many banks offer digital statements, which are not only environmentally friendly, but also easily accessible through your online banking portal – just be sure to remember your login details. All in all, managing a bank account responsibly sets the foundation for good financial habits.

Saving money might seem challenging, especially when you're young and tempted to spend on whatever takes your fancy. Even small amounts though, saved up regularly, can add up significantly over time. Another way to view it is as an emergency fund. It's like a financial safety net for unexpected expenses like medical bills or urgent repairs. Another reason to save is for larger purchases, which require more substantial amounts of money.

Understanding interest rates and how they work can also motivate you to save. Interest is the money the bank pays you for keeping your funds in a savings account. Compound interest, where you earn interest on your initial deposit and the interest it creates, can significantly increase your savings over time.

To save effectively, setting up automatic transfers to your savings account can be a simple and easy trick to get saving. This strategy takes the decision out of your hands and ensures that a portion of your income goes directly into savings. For instance, if you receive a weekly allowance or paycheck, you can set up an automatic transfer of a certain percentage to your savings account. Saving a percentage of all of your income means, with very little effort on your part, the amount you allocate to a savings account is increasing as you earn more.

Practical Tips for Building Savings

So why not making saving a habit rather than a chore. Here are some tips to get you started:

1. **Set up Automatic Transfers:** As mentioned above, automate a portion of your income to go directly into your savings account.
2. **Save a Percentage of All Income:** Aim to save a specific

percentage, like 10% of all money you receive, rather than a fixed amount.

3. **Use Savings Apps and Tools:** Use budgeting and savings apps designed for teens, such as Copper or Greenlight, which offer features tailored to young savers.

Getting to know the different types of bank accounts and the perks of saving can be your first step towards financial freedom. By opening and handling a bank account wisely and using smart saving tips, you'll be well on your way to building a strong financial future. It's like setting up your financial game plan—get ready to play and win.

1.3 THE BASICS OF CREDIT AND CREDIT SCORES

Understanding credit well is like having the keys to candy store, but it's crucial to understand exactly how it operates before diving in and taking your fill.

Let's start with the basics; credit essentially means borrowing money from a lender with the agreement to repay it later, often with interest. There are two main types of credit: credit cards and loans.

A credit card allows you to borrow money up to a limit set by the card issuer (this is the bank in most cases), which you can use for daily expenses or larger purchases. Loans, such as student loans or car loans, provide a lump sum of money that you repay over a set period. Both involve the concept of borrowing and repaying, which is fundamental to understanding how credit works. When you borrow money, you commit to paying back the original amount you borrowed (the principal) plus any interest, which is the cost of borrowing. The details of how you repay—like the interest rates and the repayment period—can differ based on the type of credit and the lender.

Credit scores play a vital role in this regard. A credit score is a three-digit number that represents whether a financial institution deems it worthy to lend you money; essentially a measure of how risky it is for them.

This score ranges from 300 to 850, with higher scores being the best. In fact, they are calculated based on several components, including how successfully you make payments, i.e. no late payments, which accounts for about 35% of your score. So, it's best to pay your bills on time. Another significant factor is how you use your credit; that's to say, the ratio of your current credit card balances to your credit limits. Keeping this ratio low, ideally below 30%, can positively impact your score.

Let's put it another way. Imagine a child has 10 toy cars, but their parents say they can only play with 3 at a time. If the child plays with fewer cars, maybe just 1 or 2, the parents are happy because the child isn't using too many toys. But if the child uses all 3 cars or tries to play with even more, the parents start to get a little concerned. Essentially, this tells the borrower that you've careful with money.

Other components may include the length of your credit history, the types of credit you use, and recent inquiries into your credit – like a credit check (amazing right? A credit check can affect your credit score!).

A good credit score can help you secure loans with favorable interest rates, rent an apartment, and even land a job, as some employers check credit scores during the hiring process.

Conversely, a bad credit score can limit your financial options and make borrowing more expensive. Therefore, regularly checking your credit score is essential to ensure accuracy and find room for improvement.

Doing all this from a young age sets the foundation for financial stability. One of the first steps is to use a credit card responsibly. This means charging only what you can afford to pay off in full each month, avoiding interest charges, and demonstrating good borrowing habits.

That's to say – make your payments on time as late payments can significantly damage your credit score and often incur late fees – it's like a viscous circle. Consider setting up automatic payments or reminders to ensure you never miss a payment that's due.

Remember, even with the best intentions, it's easy to fall into common credit traps.

Additionally, if you owe a lot of money compared to how much you're allowed to borrow, it tells lenders that you might be taking on too much and could have trouble paying it back. This makes you seem like a riskier person to lend money to. As already mentioned above, another mistake to avoid is applying for too much credit at once. Each application results in a hard inquiry into your credit score, which can lower it, all without you being too involved. Too many inquiries in a short period can make you appear desperate for credit, which is a red flag for lenders.

So, to sum up, managing credit is a crucial life skill that opens doors. But, it has to be used responsibly – make timely payments, keep how much credit you actually allow yourself to use reasonable, and build that credit by showing you can pay back what you say you can. Therefore, stick to monitoring your credit score and this will help you maintain good credit and secure your financial future.

1.4 NAVIGATING TAXES AND FILING RETURNS

As Benjamin Franklin said, "In this world, nothing is certain except death and taxes" – and, of course, it's true. Yet taxes often seem overly complicated, especially for young adults stepping into the world of personal finance.

Understanding the basics of taxes is crucial because they affect various aspects of personal finances, from your paycheck to the cost of goods. To start with the fundamentals, taxes are necessary for funding public services such as schools, roads, and emergency services. They come in different types: federal, state, and local. Let's break this down further: Federal taxes are collected by the IRS and fund national programs, while state and local taxes support regional and community services.

The concept of taxable income is central to understanding taxes. It's essentially just the portion of your income that is subject to tax, which includes wages, salaries, bonuses, and other earnings. Common tax forms you might encounter include the W-2, which reports your annual wages and the amount of taxes withheld, and the 1099, used for various types of income like freelance work or interest from savings accounts. So you can see that, basically, various incomes are accounted for here

Filing a tax return might sound dull from the outset, but breaking it down into manageable steps can make the process smoother and simpler. Let's see how it's done. Start by gathering all the necessary documents. You'll need forms like the W-2 from your employer and any 1099 forms if you have other sources of income as mentioned above. It's also helpful to keep receipts for deductible expenses, such as charitable donations or certain educational costs. Once you have all your documents, choose the right tax filing method. Online software can be a convenient option, offering step-by-step guidance and even calculating your refund or amount owed. Seeking professional help is another route, especially if your tax situation is complex. Key deadlines to remember include April 15th for filing federal and most state tax returns. Missing these deadlines can result in penalties and interest, so jot it down in your calendar and plan accordingly.

Understanding tax deductions and credits can significantly reduce your tax liability – i.e. the amount you have to pay. Tax deductions lower your taxable income, which in turn reduces the amount of tax you owe. Common deductions for teens might include educational expenses, such as tuition and textbooks, or charitable donations. On the other hand, tax credits directly reduce the amount of tax you owe – these are essentially like coupons that give you a certain amount off what was the original price. For example, the Earned Income Tax Credit (EITC) benefits low to moderate-income earners, while education credits can help offset the costs of higher education. Knowing the difference between deductions and credits is vital because they impact your taxes in different ways and can lead to significant savings.

Something else we have to be aware of is the chance of errors in the information we submit, and therefore possible penalties. Double-checking your information before submitting your tax return can prevent common mistakes, such as incorrect Social Security numbers or mismatched income amounts. Keeping organized records throughout the year can make tax season less stressful. Store important documents in a designated folder, whether physical or digital, to ensure you have everything you need when it's time to grab a coffee and get your hands dirty with paperwork. The penalties system, though it may seem harsh, encourages citizens to be thorough, which, when you think about it, benefits everyone. The IRS imposes penalties for late filing, late payment, and underpayment of taxes, which can add up quickly if not kept in check. Therefore, accuracy and being punctual are key to avoiding unnecessary fees.

Let's summarize:

- **Understanding**: Taxes might seem complicated, but knowing how they work makes them easier to handle.
- **Importance**: Being good with taxes helps set you up for future financial success.
- **Key Concepts**: Learn about different types of taxes and what taxable income is.
- **Filing Process**: Follow a clear guide to collect documents and choose how to file. Make use of step-by-step guides which are readily available.
- **Deductions vs. Credits:** Know the difference to reduce how much you owe.
- **Avoid Mistakes:** Be careful to avoid errors and penalties to keep your finances in order.

In closing, while taxes may not top everyone's list of things that bring joy, they are a crucial part of life. Taking the time to understand and manage your taxes not only fulfills a duty as a citizen – something which we should all be proud of, in fact - but it also positions you in a financially stable position. With this knowledge, you'll be better equipped to face the challenges of adulthood, ensuring that you're prepared for whatever comes your way. Remember, the skills you develop now will serve you throughout your life, making you more confident and capable in managing your finances.

CHAPTER TWO

HEALTHY COOKING SKILLS

Let's just say, for me personally, I didn't quite take to cooking. I remember looking around the kitchen after the first time I tried it on my own, and, well, it looked like a bomb had gone off. I had no idea what half of the tools were for, and I ended up burning the pasta while chopping vegetables with a dull knife. It was a mess! That being said, it taught me the importance of knowing my way around the kitchen and I'm now super proud that I got to grips with it. At the end of the day, cooking is more than just following a recipe; it's about understanding the tools and techniques that make it all possible. This chapter will guide you through the basics, from essential kitchen tools to safety tips, ensuring you're well-prepared to cook with confidence. Let's get chopping!

2.1 ESSENTIAL KITCHEN TOOLS AND SAFETY

To start cooking, you need a few essential tools that will make your life easier from the get go. These tools aren't just for fancy chefs; they are the basics that every kitchen should have. A chef's knife is probably the most important tool. It's versatile and can be used for chopping, slicing, and dicing. An 8-inch chef's knife is a good size to start with. Alongside the knife, you need a sturdy cutting board. Wooden boards made from materials like walnut or bamboo are excellent because they are gentle on your knives and can be easily cleaned. Avoid glass or plastic boards; they can dull your knives quickly.

Measuring cups and spoons are next on the list. They ensure you get the right amount of whatever you are cooking with, which is crucial for the success of any recipe – very few beginners can get it right by just guessing the amounts. A good set of measuring cups includes both dry and liquid measures. For liquids, something like a Pyrex measuring cup works well because it's microwave-safe.

Mixing bowls can make everything just that much easier. You'll need them for combining ingredients, marinating, and even serving. Stainless steel or glass bowls are durable and easy to clean too, while plastic can stain after a time.

Last on our list is having a range of pots and pans. A large pot for boiling pasta, a medium saucepan for sauces, and a skillet for frying are all good initial buys. Stainless steel and non-stick options are both useful, depending on the dish you're preparing.

Let's talk about proper use of kitchen equipment, as this not only means being safe but also ensuring that your tools last as long as they can.

For starters – excuse the pun - a chef's knife should always be sharp. A dull knife is more dangerous because it requires more force to cut, increasing the risk of slipping and cutting yourself. Sharpen your knife regularly and store it in a knife block or magnetic strip to keep the blade in good condition – best to avoid just throwing it in the drawer. Cutting boards should be cleaned thoroughly to avoid cross-contamination, especially when switching between raw meat and vegetables. Hot, soapy water or a diluted bleach solution works well for this. Some people even opt for numerous chopping boards which are color coded so you never use the same one for say veg and meat.

It's important to have fun, but we should always consider how to stay safe. Handling knives safely is a top priority, for instance. Always cut away from your body and keep your fingers tucked in to avoid accidents – the shape is the same as when you're grabbing on to a door handle. Use a stable cutting board to prevent it from slipping too – you can put a tea-towel underneath if you're worried about this. When it comes to preventing burns and scalding, always use oven mitts or pot holders when handling hot pots and pans. Turn pot handles inward on the stove to avoid knocking them over when you pass by. Flammable items like paper towels and dishcloths should be kept away from the stove to prevent fires. Knowing where your fire extinguisher is and how to use it can also be lifesaving, and, of course, if you don't have one of these, it's probably a good time to invest.

Also, as hard as we may try to avoid them, accidents do happen, so it's essential to know some basic first aid for common kitchen injuries. For minor cuts, rinse the wound under cool water and apply pressure with a clean cloth to stop the bleeding. Once the bleeding has stopped, apply an antiseptic cream and cover the cut with a bandage. For burns, cool the area under running water for at least 10 minutes and then cover it with a sterile, non-stick dressing. Avoid using ice, as it can damage the skin further. If you fall, assess your injuries first before trying to get up and if you're dizzy or in severe pain, seek help immediately.

Cooking is more than just making food—it's about having fun and being safe in the kitchen. With the right tools, good upkeep, and some safety tips, you'll soon feel like a pro.

2.2 COOKING SIMPLE AND NUTRITIOUS MEALS

Cooking your own meals can be incredibly satisfying and fun. It's a skill that not only saves money but also allows you to control what goes into your body. Understanding basic cooking techniques is the first step in becoming a competent cook. Let's go through some of the main processes: boiling and steaming are great for making vegetables and grains like rice or quinoa. I would personally recommend steaming, if it's an option – it can't be used with grains for example. I say this because it is a way of preserving more nutrients. Sautéing and stir-frying involve cooking food quickly in a small amount of oil over high heat. This technique is excellent for vegetables, meats, and even tofu. Baking is often used for breads and pastries – while roasting is perfect for meats and vegetables, giving them a deliciously crispy exterior; both make use a hot oven.

. . .

Well, I'm sure you're eager to get going, so here are some easy-to-follow recipes that you can try on your own.

For breakfast, oatmeal with fruits and nuts is a nutritious and quick option. Start by boiling water or milk and then add rolled oats. Cook for about five minutes, stirring occasionally; once the oats are cooked, top with a handful of fresh or dried fruits like berries or raisins and some nuts, such as almonds or walnuts. This meal provides a good balance of carbohydrates, fiber, and healthy fats.

For lunch, a grilled chicken salad is both tasty and filling. Season a chicken breast with salt, pepper and add your favorite herbs (you might not know just yet which ones you prefer, but get buying and experiment), then grill until fully cooked. Slice the chicken and toss it with mixed greens, cherry tomatoes, cucumber, and a vinaigrette made of olive oil, vinegar, and a pinch of salt. This salad offers lean protein, vitamins, and healthy fats.

For dinner, pasta with marinara sauce and vegetables is one of my go-to meals. Cook whole-grain pasta according to the instructions on the pack. In a separate pan, sauté chopped onions, garlic, and bell peppers in a bit of olive oil. Add a jar of marinara sauce and let it simmer. Mix the cooked pasta with the sauce and vegetables, and you have a balanced meal rich in carbohydrates, fiber, and vitamins.

. . .

As the recipes above attest to, you should look to make your meals balanced. Each meal should include a mix of protein, carbohydrates, and fats. Protein helps build and repair tissues, carbohydrates provide energy, and fats are essential for absorbing vitamins. Alongside my examples above, a balanced meal might include a piece of grilled fish (protein), a serving of quinoa (carbohydrates), and a side of avocado (healthy fats). Portion control is also important to avoid overeating. Use smaller plates, and fill half of your plate with vegetables, a quarter with protein, and the remaining quarter with carbohydrates. This way of visualizing your dish can help you maintain a balanced diet without having to measure everything precisely.

Adjusting recipes to meet dietary needs is easier than you might think; in the case where you need gluten-free options, use gluten-free pasta or buy specially-made bread – there have never been so many options, not just in specialty stores, but in your local super-market. Many recipes can be easily adapted by substituting gluten-free grains like rice or quinoa too. For those following a vegetarian or vegan diet, there are plenty of plant-based protein sources like beans, lentils, and tofu. Why not, instead of using chicken in your salad, add chickpeas or grilled tofu. Low-sugar alternatives are also available for those watching their sugar intake. Use natural sweeteners like honey or maple syrup in moderation or go for fruits to add sweetness to your dishes. This way, you can enjoy delicious meals that match your dietary preferences and restrictions without compromising on taste or nutrition.

· · ·

I hope you've seen that it needn't be complicated or time-consuming. By mastering basic cooking techniques and understanding how to create balanced meals, you can enjoy the process of cooking as well as the sitting down and eating. Whether you're making oatmeal for breakfast, a salad for lunch, or pasta for dinner, these skills will serve you well, helping you stay healthy and satisfied.

2.3 READING AND UNDERSTANDING NUTRITION LABELS

Many of us take a while to get into this habit, but once you get the hang of it, these become incredibly useful tools for making healthier food choices. The first thing to look at is the serving size and the number of servings per container, packet, tin etc. In fact, these are important because they relate directly to the nutritional information. For example, if a bag of chips lists 150 calories per serving and has 3 servings per container, eating the entire bag means consuming 450 calories. This information ultimately helps you manage portion sizes and avoid overeating.

Next, focus on the calories and macronutrients. The most important of these are calories; they indicate the energy you get from one serving of the food. Keeping an eye on calorie intake is important for maintaining a healthy weight. The macronutrients —protein, fat, and carbohydrates—are listed next on the pack. Protein is essential for building and repairing tissues, while fats and carbohydrates provide energy. Pay attention to the types of fat listed as well; you'll often see saturated fats and trans fats (or, trans fatty acids). Saturated fat should be limited, and trans fat is best avoided altogether. Carbohydrates include sugars and fiber. Fiber is beneficial for digestion and can make you feel full for longer – so this is highly prized, while sugars should be consumed in moderation. You should be able to find this on most packets.

Key nutrients like vitamins and minerals are also listed on the label. These are crucial for various bodily functions. For instance, calcium is vital for bone health, while iron is necessary to keep blood functioning properly. The label also shows the percentage of the daily value (%DV) for each nutrient, based on a 2,000-calorie diet. This percentage helps you understand how much of your daily nutrient needs are met by one serving of the food. For example, if a serving of cereal provides 20% of the daily value for calcium, you know it's a good source of that nutrient.

It falls on you to look out for possibly harmful ingredients and think about how you can avoid these, or consume them in moderation. Added sugars are a big one. These are sugars not naturally occurring in the food and can contribute to weight gain and other health issues. Look for terms like high fructose corn syrup, dextrose, or sucrose. As mentioned above, trans fats are another ingredient to avoid. These are often found in processed foods and can increase the risk of heart disease. Check for partially hydrogenated oils in the ingredients list too. Artificial additives and preservatives are also red flags. These can include substances like artificial colors, flavors, and preservatives such as sodium benzoate or nitrates, which have been linked to various health conditions. Why not head to the kitchen now and have a good look over the labels and see if you can spot some of these? Why not categorize the packs in two piles: healthy and non-healthy? You might be surprised what ends up getting tossed into the non-healthy pile.

. . .

Comparing food products can help you make healthier choices. For instance, when choosing cereals, take the time to compare the sugar content, as some cereals can have as much sugar as a candy bar, while others offer more fiber and less sugar and so are a better option overall. Look for cereals with at least 3 grams of fiber and less than 10 grams of sugar per serving. Evaluating snack options is similar. Choose snacks that offer nutritional benefits like added fiber and protein, rather than empty calories from sugars and fats. For example, compare a bag of chips with a serving of nuts. Nuts might be higher in calories, but they provide healthy fats and protein, making them a more nutritious choice.

Health claims on food packaging can be confusing. Terms like "low-fat" and "reduced-fat" sound similar but mean different things. "Low-fat" means the food contains 3 grams of fat or less per serving, while "reduced-fat" means the food has 25% less fat than the regular version. "Organic" vs. "natural" is another common area for confusion. "Organic" foods are produced without synthetic pesticides or fertilizers and usually have a certified organic label. "Natural" foods, on the other hand, are processed only minimally but are not necessarily free of synthetic ingredients. Claims like "high in fiber" mean the food provides 20% or more of the daily value for fiber per serving. Understanding these terms can help you make better choices that align with your health goals.

2.4 MEAL PLANNING AND GROCERY SHOPPING TIPS

As with so many things, planning is key. Don't feel put off by the extra effort of reaching for a notepad and listing things down that you'll need for the week. It's a lifesaver when it comes to maintaining a balanced diet, and, as an added bonus, can really help keep food waste to a minimum.

Start by planning your meals for breakfast, lunch, dinner, and snacks you'll have in between. This helps you see the bigger picture of your nutritional intake and ensures you have a variety of foods. For breakfast, you might plan oatmeal with fruits on Monday, scrambled eggs on Tuesday, and smoothies on Wednesday – thinking in terms of just one day can often lead to overly simplified meals. Lunchtime could include salads, sandwiches, and leftovers from the night before. Dinner is where you can get creative—think grilled chicken with veggies one night, pasta another, and perhaps a homemade pizza on the weekend. Don't forget snacks too; include fruits, nuts, or yogurts to keep your energy up throughout the day. Adjust your meal plan based on your activities and schedule as you need. If you have a busy week, opt for simpler meals or prepare ingredients in advance to save time.

When it comes to grocery shopping, having a strategy can save you time and money. Start by making a shopping list based on your meal plan. This ensures you only buy what you need and helps you avoid impulse purchases. Stick to the perimeter of the store where fresh produce, dairy, and lean proteins are usually located. This way, you fill your cart with healthier options first.

Compare prices and look for sales to make the most of your budget. Store brands often offer quality products at a lower price than name brands. Keep an eye out for discounts on items you frequently use, and consider stocking up if they have a long shelf life – things like flour, pasta and rice, for instance.

Planning yummy, nutritious meals on a budget doesn't mean you have to skimp on quality! You can eat well without breaking the bank! Buying in bulk is one effective strategy to stick to your budget. Items like rice, pasta, and canned goods often come at a lower cost per unit when purchased in larger quantities. Using seasonal produce is another way to save money. Seasonal fruits and vegetables are usually cheaper and fresher. For example, buy strawberries in the summer when they're at their peak and more affordable. Cooking in batches and freezing portions can also stretch your budget. Make a large pot of soup or a casserole, then freeze individual portions for later. This not only saves money but also time, as you'll have ready-to-eat meals on those busy days. Also, this will stop the temptation to order food in.

Reducing food waste is both eco-friendly and budget-conscious. Proper storage of fruits and vegetables can prolong their freshness. A good idea is to store leafy greens in a container with a paper towel to absorb excess moisture. Keep fruits like apples and bananas separate, as they produce ethylene gas that can cause other produce to ripen too quickly (although this can be good for quickly ripening an avocado). Repurposing leftovers is another smart tactic. Leftover roasted chicken can be chopped up and thrown into a salad or can make for a good sandwich filling. Vegetables from the night before can be added to a breakfast omelet. If you find yourself with food scraps, consider composting them. This not only reduces waste but also provides nutrient-rich compost for gardening – then you can grow your own veg!

I hope I've convinced you – meal planning and smart grocery shopping are fundamental skills and they ensure a balanced diet and the ability to stick to a budget. With a bit of organization and creativity, you too can enjoy nutritious meals without breaking the bank or wasting food.

Let's look back over the chapter: we've covered the essentials of healthy cooking, from understanding kitchen tools to planning meals and grocery shopping. Armed with these skills, you're better prepared to manage your nutrition and budget effectively. Next, we'll explore time management and how this can lead us to success as we develop into young adults.

CHAPTER THREE

EFFECTIVE TIME MANAGEMENT

When I was in high school, I remember feeling overwhelmed by the sheer number of tasks I had to juggle. Between homework, part-time jobs, and social activities, it seemed like there were never enough hours in the day. One particularly hectic week, I found myself staring at a pile of unfinished assignments, wondering how I could possibly get it all done. It was then that a teacher introduced me to the concept of setting SMART goals, a method that completely transformed how I managed my time and responsibilities. Want to get SMART? Read on.

3.1 SETTING SMART GOALS

Let's get to grips with the SMART goals framework, and see how it is essential for setting and achieving meaningful objectives. SMART stands for Specific, Measurable, Achievable, Relevant and Time-bound and it provides a structured approach to goal-setting, making it easier to accomplish what you set out to do. A specific goal clearly defines what you want to achieve. Instead of saying, "I want to do well in school," a specific goal would be, "I want to improve my math grade from a B to an A." This clarity gives you a precise target to aim for.

Measurable goals involve determining how you will track your progress. For example, if your goal is to improve your math grade, you might measure your progress by tracking your scores on quizzes and tests. This way, you can see clear indications of your improvement. Achievable goals are realistic and within your capability. It's important to set goals that challenge you, but are still attainable. If you're currently getting a C in math, aiming for an A might be too ambitious in a short timeframe. Instead, aim to move from a C to a B, then reassess and set a new goal. Relevant goals align with your broader objectives and priorities. If improving your math grade is important for getting into your desired college program, then it's relevant. Finally, time-bound goals have a deadline. Setting a timeframe, such as "I want to improve my math grade by the end of this semester," creates a sense of urgency and helps you stay focused – we all do better when we have a fixed date to focus on.

So, what are the steps to creating effective SMART goals.

1. Start by identifying an area where you want to see improvement. For academic goals, you might focus on subjects where you struggle. For example, if you want to improve your grades, a SMART goal could be: "I will dedicate an extra hour each week to studying math to raise my grade from a C to a B by the end of the semester." For personal goals, think about skills you

want to develop or habits you want to form. If you want to improve your fitness, a SMART goal might be: "I will jog for 30 minutes three times a week for the next two months to build my endurance." Once you've set your goals, write them down and review them regularly. This keeps them at the forefront of your mind and helps you stay committed.

2. Tracking the progress of your goals is crucial for staying on track and making adjustments as needed. Using journals or apps can help you monitor your progress. For instance, you might use a journal to log your study hours and track your quiz scores in math class. Apps like Todoist or Trello can be used for this purpose, but they may also be useful for setting up and tracking milestones related to your goals. Regular check-ins, whether weekly or monthly, allow you to assess your progress and make any necessary adjustments based on the feedback you see. If you find that you're not meeting your study hours, you can adjust your schedule or seek additional help from a teacher or tutor.

3. Overcoming obstacles is also part of the goal-setting process. It's normal to encounter setbacks, but how you respond to them can make all the difference. Seven times Formula 1 World Champion Lewis Hamilton always says, "It's not how you, it's how you pick yourself back up". Dealing with setbacks involves staying motivated and not letting failures discourage you. If you miss a study session, don't give up. Instead, find a way to make up for that lost time. Seeking support from friends, family, or mentors can also be invaluable when it comes to these challenges. They can offer encouragement, advice, and even help you stay accountable. You might find study

groups can provide a sense of companionship and motivation, making it easier to stick to your goals.

SMART goals then help you focus your efforts, track your progress, and achieve your objectives more effectively. By understanding and implementing this framework, you can turn your aspirations into a reality, whether they're academic or personal. Added to this, you'll find that such an approach builds confidence for goals you'll set yourself in the future – you can head into new challenges knowing that you've already been there and done it before.

3.2 PRIORITIZING TASKS AND AVOIDING PROCRASTINATION

How good are you at identifying priorities? Can you tell the difference between something requiring immediate attention now or if it's okay to leave it for a few days? One effective method to help you sort through and prioritize tasks is the Eisenhower Matrix. This tool, named after President Dwight D. Eisenhower, categorizes tasks into four quadrants: urgent and important, important but not urgent, urgent but not important, and neither urgent nor important. By dividing tasks this way, you can quickly identify what needs immediate attention and what can wait. Let's look at what might be a common example for many teens: finishing a school project due tomorrow would fall into the urgent and important category, while planning a study schedule for next month might be important but not urgent.

Managing tasks effectively involves breaking down large tasks into smaller, manageable steps – sometimes called the bite size approach. This approach reduces the feeling of being overwhelmed and makes it easier to start – i.e. a small bite, rather than a huge mouthful. Suppose you have a major research paper due; instead of seeing it as one massive task, break it down into smaller steps like choosing a topic, gathering sources, drafting an outline, writing sections, and revising. Using to-do lists and task management tools can help you stay organized in this regard. Apps like Todoist or Trello, which I've already mentioned above, offer visual boards and lists that can be customized to fit your needs. Setting deadlines for each step ensures you stay on track and complete tasks on time.

Understanding procrastination is crucial for tackling it head-on. Procrastination often stems from a fear of failure, perfectionism, or lack of motivation. Fear of failure can paralyze you, making it easier for you to put off starting a task than to risk not doing it well. Perfectionism, the need to perform tasks flawlessly, can also lead to delays because you might spend too much time on minor details. A lack of motivation might also come from finding the task uninteresting or overwhelming. Recognizing these under-lying reasons can help you develop strategies to combat them.

One practical strategy to overcome procrastination is the Pomodoro Technique, which involves working in short bursts followed by breaks. Interestingly, Pomodoro is the Italian word for "Tomato"; Francesco Cirillo, the inventor is said to have used a kitchen timer shaped like a tomato when he first came up with this idea – and, well, the name has stuck. Set a timer for 25 minutes – either tomato shaped or not - and focus on a single task. When the timer goes off, take a five-minute break. After four cycles, take a longer break. This method can boost your focus and productivity by making the work time manageable and the breaks restorative. YouTube has many Pomodoro timers set up and ready to use of varying lengths. Setting up a reward system can also help. Promise yourself a small treat, like a favorite snack or a short game break, after completing a task. This creates positive reinforcement and makes the task more enjoyable.

Creating a distraction-free work environment is another key to staying on track. Start by organizing your workspace. Keep only the materials you need for the task at hand. Proper lighting and a comfy desk can also make a big difference. A well-lit space with a nice, solid chair and desk setup can improve focus and reduce fatigue. Removing potential distractions, like turning off your phone or blocking social media sites during work time, can help you stay focused. If you find it hard to disconnect, apps like Forest can lock you out of distracting sites while you work, rewarding you with a virtual tree that grows as you stay focused. It's actually very cute – trust me!

Interactive Element: Prioritization Exercise

Why not take a few minutes to list all the tasks you need to complete this week? Use the Eisenhower Matrix to categorize them into the four quadrants. Once you've sorted your tasks, choose one urgent and important task to tackle first. Break it down into smaller steps and set deadlines for each. Reflect on how this exercise helps you feel more organized and in control of your workload.

• • •

By figuring out your priorities, managing tasks better, and understanding why you procrastinate (plus using smart strategies to tackle it), you're guaranteed to boost your productivity and feel less stressed. These skills will not only make school smoother but also set you up for success in your future career and personal life, helping you stay more balanced and effective overall.

3.3 CREATING A DAILY AND WEEKLY SCHEDULE

Having a structured daily and weekly schedule can be a great way to manage your time effectively. One of the biggest benefits is the reduction of stress and anxiety – something I'm sure all of us want to limit. When you have a clear plan for your day or week, you know exactly what needs to be done and when. This eliminates the constant worry of forgetting something important or running out of time. A good schedule also ensures a balanced lifestyle. It allows you to allocate time for school, homework, extracurricular activities, and relaxation, making sure you don't overdo it and fall short in any other aspects of your life, like, say, keeping fit. Improved productivity and focus are other key advantages. When you know what tasks you need to complete and have set times for them, you can concentrate better and get more done; it's like waking up every day with a purpose.

Designing a daily schedule that takes into account all necessary activities involves a few simple steps. Start by listing everything you need to do in a day, including school, homework, extracurricular activities, and downtime. Allocate specific time slots for each activity. For example, you might dedicate 3:00 PM to 4:30 PM for homework, 5:00 PM to 6:00 PM for sports practice, and 7:00 PM to 8:00 PM for relaxation. Make sure to include breaks and allow for some flexibility. Life is unpredictable, and sometimes things don't go as planned. Having a little wiggle room in your schedule can help you adapt without feeling overwhelmed.

Planning a weekly schedule helps manage long-term projects and responsibilities more effectively. Start by identifying the major tasks and goals for the week. Allocate time for different subjects or activities, ensuring you're not overloaded on any given day. Take for example you have a big project due at the end of the week, break it down into smaller tasks and spread them out over several days. Set specific goals for each week, such as finishing the first draft of a paper by Wednesday or studying for a test on Friday. Reviewing and adjusting your schedule as needed is crucial. At the end of each week, take a few minutes to assess what worked and what didn't. Make any necessary changes to improve your schedule for the following week – we can't all be expected to get it right, first go.

Using scheduling tools can make creating and managing your schedule much easier. Digital calendars like Google Calendar or Apple Calendar are excellent for setting up reminders and keeping track of appointments and deadlines. These tools allow you to sync your schedule across multiple devices, ensuring you always have access to it. If you prefer a more traditional approach, a paper planner or bullet journal can also be very effective. These methods allow for a more personalized touch and can be a great way to reflect on your day or week. I personally love a good post-it-note.

. . .

Creating a daily and weekly schedule that works for you takes a bit of practice, but the perks are well worth it. A well-structured schedule can reduce stress, ensure a balanced lifestyle, and improve your productivity and focus. By following these steps and using the right tools, you can take control of your time and make the most of each day.

3.4 TECHNIQUES FOR STAYING FOCUSED AND PRODUCTIVE

One nice way to enhance your focus and productivity is to take a look at where you do your work as this can often signal where there might be issues. Start by organizing your workspace. A clutter-free desk can help clear your mind and improve concentration. Store away unnecessary items and keep only the essentials within reach. Proper lighting is crucial, too. Natural light is the best, so position your desk near a window if possible. If you rely on artificial light, opt for a bright, white light that mimics daylight. Ergonomics - the science of designing work environments and systems to maximize human well-being, comfort, and performance - play a major role in your efficiency. Use a chair that supports your lower back – often called Lumbar support - and make sure your computer screen is at eye level to avoid neck strain. Finally, remove potential distractions. Turn off notifications on your phone or place it in another room. Blocking social media sites during work hours can also make a significant difference. Again, there are plenty of apps to do this, or you'll find that your phone even has settings to help you achieve this; Android for instance has *modes*, which you can find in the settings.

Time management techniques can further enhance your ability to stay focused. We've already mentioned the Pomodoro technique, but what about Time Blocking? This is essentially a way to dedi-cate specific time slots to different tasks throughout your day. You can think of it this way; allocate 9:00 AM to 11:00 AM for study-ing, then switch to other activities, i.e. work in blocks. This method is guaranteed to help you stay committed to each task without getting sidetracked. The two-minute rule, promoted in James Clear's wonderful book *Atomic Habits*, is a simple yet powerful technique: it simply states that, if a task takes less than two minutes to complete, do it immediately. This prevents small tasks from piling up and becoming overwhelming. Loading the dishwasher, taking your daily vitamins, watering the plants on your windowsill – there are hundreds of such tasks that are neces-sary, but really don't take very much time at all to get done.

If you're like me, you might struggle to keep your energy levels up through the day. But don't worry, I've got some hacks. Regular breaks are crucial. Short breaks during work sessions help rejuve-nate your mind and body. Stand up, stretch, or take a quick walk to keep your energy levels up. Eating nutritious snacks can also make a big difference. Choose foods that provide sustained energy, such as nuts, fruits, and yogurt, rather than sugary snacks that might feel good at first, but will soon lead to crashes. Staying hydrated is equally important. Dehydration can negatively impact your focus and cognitive functions, so keep a water bottle nearby and take regular sips. Aim for at least eight glasses of water per day to stay adequately hydrated. Of course, there are apps for this too, like WaterMinder – there's an app for everything!

Building productive habits over time can lead to long-term success. Establishing a consistent daily routine lays the foundation of productive habits. Start your day with a morning routine that sets a positive tone, such as a brief workout, a healthy breakfast, and setting your goals for the day. Setting up accountability systems can also help maintain these habits. Join a study group or find a productivity partner who shares similar goals. Regular check-ins and mutual support can keep you motivated and on track. It's always a great idea to reflect on your progress and make adjustments. At the end of each week, review what worked and what didn't – it's okay if something didn't work out – remember the words of Lewis Hamilton, "It's how you pick yourself back up".

So, let's summarize exactly what we've learnt here:

- Boost focus and productivity with simple daily techniques
- Set up a work environment that helps you stay on task
- Use smart time management to keep things moving
- Keep your energy up throughout the day
- Build habits that make reaching your goals easier

Doesn't sound so difficult, right? Let's move on to another key area, especially focused on 'care of the self'.

CHAPTER FOUR

PERSONAL HYGIENE AND GROOMING

I remember a moment during my middle school years when I was getting ready for a big school event. My mom handed me a stick of deodorant and said, "You'll thank me later." At the time, I didn't fully grasp the importance of maintaining good hygiene. But as I grew older, I realized it wasn't just about smelling nice; it was about feeling confident and making a positive impression. Personal hygiene helps us stay healthy and feel great around others, and it changes as we go through different stages of life. Let's explore further how to get to grips with it.

4.1 DAILY HYGIENE ROUTINES

There are several reasons to get on top of this from the get go. First and foremost, it helps prevent illness and infections. Our bodies come into contact with countless germs and bacteria every day, and without proper hygiene, these can lead to various health issues. For instance, washing your hands regularly can reduce the risk of catching colds or stomach bugs. It's not only this, though; good hygiene actually boosts our self-esteem. When you feel clean and fresh, you naturally feel more confident. This confidence extends to your social interactions, helping you make a good impression on others. Whether you're meeting new friends, going on a date, or attending a job interview, good hygiene can make a significant difference in how you're perceived by other, and how you perceive yourself.

Starting your day with a thorough hygiene routine is a must. Begin with brushing and flossing your teeth. Dentists recommend brushing for at least two minutes, covering all areas of the mouth to remove plaque and prevent cavities. Use fluoride toothpaste and replace your toothbrush every three months; better still, why not opt for an electric toothbrush – many of them have timers integrated so you know you're brushing effectively. Flossing is equally important as it removes food particles and plaque between your teeth that brushing alone can't reach. After dental care, move on to washing your face. Use a gentle cleanser suitable for your skin type to remove dirt and excess oil. Pat your face dry with a clean towel and apply deodorant to keep body odor at bay throughout the day. In the evening, repeat the dental care routine and wash your face again or take a shower to remove any impurities accumulated during the day. This routine helps maintain healthy skin and teeth, ensuring you feel and look your best.

Hand hygiene plays a critical role in preventing the spread of germs. Proper handwashing techniques involve using soap and water, scrubbing your hands all over, including the backs, between the fingers, and under the nails, for at least 20 seconds. Some like to hum the tune of Happy Birthday – this being more or less 20 seconds in length. Always wash your hands before meals, after using the restroom, and after coming into contact with potentially dirty surfaces. If soap and water aren't available, use hand sanitizer with at least 60% alcohol content. This helps kill most germs and provides a convenient alternative when you're on the go. Consistent hand hygiene reduces your risk of illness and keeps those around you healthier too – it's a win-win.

Body hygiene is equally important. Regular bathing helps remove sweat, dirt, and dead skin cells, preventing body odor and skin infections. Aim to shower daily, especially after physical activities. Use a mild soap and shampoo to cleanse your body and hair. Pay attention to areas prone to sweating, such as the underarms and groin, to prevent odors. Cleaning under your nails with a nail brush during your shower ensures that dirt and bacteria are removed, reducing the risk of infections. After showering, dry yourself thoroughly to prevent fungal infections, particularly in areas like between your toes.

Good hygiene habits developed during adolescence can lay the foundation for a lifetime of health and confidence. Looking good is just part of it; feeling good and presenting yourself well are equally important. Engaging in daily hygiene routines, practicing proper hand hygiene, and maintaining body cleanliness are simple yet powerful tools towards achieving this goal.

4.2 SKINCARE BASICS AND TIPS

Understanding your skin type is perhaps the first step in creating an effective skincare routine. Skin types generally fall into four categories: oily, dry, combination, and sensitive. Oily skin tends to produce excess sebum, making it shiny and prone to acne. You might notice larger pores and frequent breakouts. Dry skin, on the other hand, lacks moisture and can feel tight or flaky. It often appears dull and may have visible lines. Combination skin has both oily and dry areas, typically with an oily T-zone (forehead, nose, and chin) and dry cheeks. Sensitive skin reacts easily to products or environmental factors, leading to redness, itching, or irritation. Have a think now about which category you may fall into; doing this can ensure better results overall as you are buying products tailored to your skin type.

A simple and effective daily skincare routine can work wonders for your skin. Start with cleansing. Choose a gentle cleanser to remove dirt and excess oil without stripping your skin of its natural moisture. For oily or acne-prone skin, a gel-based cleanser works well. For dry or sensitive skin, opt for a creamy, hydrating cleanser. After cleansing, use a toner to balance your skin's pH and remove any leftover impurities. Toning prepares your skin for the following steps and can help tighten pores. Next, think about how best to moisturize. Even oily skin needs moisture to prevent the overproduction of oil. Look for a lightweight, non-comedo-genic moisturizer if you have oily skin, and a richer, more hydrating one for dry skin. Finally, never skip sun protection. Using SPF daily protects your skin from harmful UV rays, preventing premature aging and reducing the risk of skin cancer. Choose a broad-spectrum sunscreen with at least SPF 30 and apply it every morning, even on cloudy days.

Dealing with common skin issues like acne and blackheads can be frustrating, but there are effective ways to manage them. Over-the-counter treatments often include ingredients like salicylic acid or benzoyl peroxide, which help reduce acne by unclogging pores and killing bacteria. Apply these treatments to the affected areas after cleansing and before moisturizing. Natural remedies can also be beneficial. Tea tree oil has antibacterial properties and can be applied to pimples to reduce inflammation. Honey masks can soothe the skin and provide antibacterial benefits. However, it's important to know when to seek professional help. If over-the-counter treatments and natural remedies don't work, or if your acne is severe, consult a dermatologist as they can provide prescription treatments or procedures that address your specific skin concerns more effectively.

Oddly enough, staying hydrated is also vital for maintaining skin health. Drinking plenty of water helps flush out toxins and keeps your skin looking plump and hydrated. As mentioned in a previous section, aim for at least eight glasses of water a day. Eating a balanced diet rich in vitamins and minerals also contributes to healthy skin. Foods high in antioxidants, like fruits and vegetables, protect your skin from damage. Omega-3 fatty acids found in fish and flaxseeds can help keep your skin moisturized as well. Getting enough sleep is also massively important. Lack of sleep can lead to dull skin and dark circles under your eyes. Aim for 7-9 hours of quality sleep each night to allow your skin to repair and regenerate.

Thinking about and taking seriously these skincare basics and tips can make a significant difference in your skin's appearance and health, which can ultimately boost your confidence too. Understanding your skin type, following a consistent routine, managing common skin issues, and adopting healthy skin habits are all essential steps towards achieving clear, glowing skin. You might want to reflect on how you currently feel about the appearance of your skin, whether you're suffering any of issues mentioned above and think about how you can best find solutions.

4.3 HAIR CARE AND STYLING

You might be one of those obsessives when it comes to hair, or it might not even be a factor for you. Either way, it's always good to think about how best to keep it looking good and ready to impress when the time comes. Let's start with types of hair; these generally fall into four categories: straight, wavy, curly, and coily. Straight hair tends to be sleek and can get oily quickly because natural oils travel down the shafts of the hairs more easily. It often requires lightweight products to avoid looking greasy. Wavy hair has a natural, tousled texture that can range from loose waves to more defined ones. It often benefits from light mousses or gels that enhance the waviness without weighing it down. Curly hair forms distinct curls and can range from loose ringlets to tight spirals. It usually needs extra moisture to combat frizz and maintain the natural curls. Coily hair, characterized by tight curls or coils, is the most fragile and requires rich, hydrating products to keep it healthy and defined. Take a moment to think about what type you have and what products you currently use to manage your hairdo.

There are just a few essential steps to consider and they are easy to add into your daily routine. Choosing the right shampoo and conditioner is top of the list. For straight and oily hair, opt for a clarifying shampoo that removes excess oil without stripping the hair of its natural moisture. For dry or curly hair, a moisturizing shampoo and conditioner can help retain hydration. Always follow up with a conditioner tailored to your hair type. Brushing techniques also vary by hair type. Straight hair can be brushed while dry to distribute oils evenly. For wavy and curly hair, it's best to detangle while wet using a wide-tooth comb, which also avoids breakages and frizzing. Coily hair benefits from gentle finger detangling or using a wide-tooth comb with plenty of conditioner to prevent damage. Try not to use too much equipment which heats up the hair. It can in fact weaken hair, leading to breakage and split ends. If you must use heat tools, always apply a heat protectant spray first and use the lowest temperature setting that still remains effective.

You should think of your hair as an extension of you – your personality. You can have a lot of fun with it. For straight hair, adding volume can make a big difference for example. Use a volumizing mousse at the roots before blow-drying to lift the hair and create fullness. Curly hair requires techniques that define curls without causing frizz. After washing, apply a curl-enhancing cream or gel while your hair is still wet. Scrunch the product into your curls and let your hair air dry or use a diffuser. Protective styles are particularly beneficial for textured and coily hair. Braids, twists, and buns not only look stylish but also help you to protect your hair from the daily dirt and grime and it means less effort overall. These styles can even help retain length and minimize breakage, keeping your hair healthy and stronger.

. . .

Do you go to the salon or the barbers once a week or once a year? How often you need a haircut depends on your hair type and personal preference. Generally, getting a trim every 6-8 weeks helps remove split ends and keeps your hair looking fresh, although some with short hair simply like to keep it that way, and they may go every two weeks or so. Alongside a regular cut, you might want to consider deep conditioning treatments, which can be done at home and can make a significant difference, especially for dry or damaged hair. Use a deep conditioner or hair mask once a week to nourish and strengthen your hair. Scalp care is another important aspect of hair health. A healthy scalp promotes hair growth and prevents issues like dandruff. Use a gentle exfoliating scrub once a month to remove dead skin cells and buildup. Massage your scalp regularly to stimulate blood flow and keep it healthy.

Knowing your hair type and sticking to a simple care routine can really improve how your hair looks and feels. Using the right products, brushing gently, and avoiding too much heat styling are all important steps. Regular trims and looking after your scalp help keep your hair healthy and shiny. Whether your hair is straight, wavy, curly, or coily, these habits will help you enhance your natural look.

4.4 DRESSING FOR DIFFERENT OCCASIONS

Of course, fashions are constantly changing, but there are often clothes that are just right for the occasion – as they often say, "Style never goes out of fashion". Dress codes vary depending on the event and setting though. Casual dress codes are the most relaxed. Think of jeans, t-shirts, and sneakers—perfect for hanging out with friends or attending a casual class. Business casual steps it up a notch. This might include khakis or dress pants paired with a nice blouse or button-down shirt. It's the go-to for school presentations or part-time job interviews. Formal attire is reserved for special occasions like weddings, proms, or formal dinners. This means suits or tuxedos for guys and elegant dresses or gowns for girls. It's often about knowing that you can accommodate to the dress code that is required and have clothing ready-to-use that you feel comfortable wearing.

Building a good wardrobe is all about having key pieces that can be mixed and matched for different occasions. Start with the essentials. A good pair of jeans is a must—comfortable, durable, and good for so many different occasions. A well-fitted blazer can instantly elevate your look, whether you're wearing it over a t-shirt for a smart-casual vibe or with dress pants for something more formal. Dress shoes are another staple. They should be comfortable enough to wear for extended periods but stylish enough to complement a variety of outfits. Think about how your clothing might adapt when choosing. A simple white shirt can be worn with jeans for a casual look or tucked into a skirt for something more formal. Layering is another great way to create different looks. A cardigan or a jacket can change the entire feel of an outfit.

So, you get an invite or you've got an event coming up – how shall we approach this in terms of dress. First, assess the occasion and setting. A family barbecue calls for a different outfit than a job interview. Consider the weather and season as well. Lightweight fabrics are ideal for summer, while layering is key in colder months. Reflecting on your personal style while adhering to the dress code is also important; if you love bold colors, find a way to incorporate them into your outfit, even if it's just through accessories. Feeling comfortable in what you wear boosts your confidence, making you more at ease in any setting. This simply requires taking a little time in front of the mirror – getting a sense of what you personally like, and what probably needs another term in the closet.

Accessorizing can be really fun and can spruce up any outfit. Watches, jewelry, and belts can add a touch of sophistication. When it comes to coordinating colors and patterns, a good rule of thumb is to stick to one or two main colors and one pattern. For instance, if you're wearing a patterned shirt, keep your pants and shoes in solid, neutral colors. You may want to consider those personal grooming final touches as well. Clean nails and polished shoes show attention to detail and can elevate your overall look.

In this chapter, we've covered everything from understanding dress codes to building a versatile wardrobe and choosing the right outfit for any occasion. These tips will help you navigate social and professional settings with confidence. Next, we'll delve into the importance of first aid and emergency preparedness, equipping you with the skills to handle unexpected situations.

CHAPTER FIVE

EMERGENCY PREPAREDNESS

A few years ago, I was babysitting my younger brother when he fell off his bike and scraped his knee badly. I panicked, unsure of what to do. That moment of helplessness made me realize the importance of knowing basic first aid and since then I've committed time and effort to learning some basics as I know they'll certainly come in handy one day. Look, emergencies can happen at any time, and being prepared can make all the difference. So, let's equip you with some of those essentials, starting with basic first aid, minor injuries and how to stay calm in a crisis.

5.1 BASIC FIRST AID SKILLS

There's been an accident! Do we need to call for help? Is there something we can all do in the meantime? Aren't there some basics that we should get to grips with? Of course there are, and knowing them can mean the difference between life and death. The first principle is to stay calm. Panicking can make the situation worse and prevent you from thinking clearly. Take a deep breath and assess the situation. Determine the severity of the injury and whether immediate medical attention is needed. Knowing when to call for professional help is a judgment call that we may all have to make one day. In cases of severe bleeding, difficulty breathing, or suspected broken bones, always dial emergency services right away.

Treating minor cuts and scrapes involves a few simple steps. First, clean the wound with soap and water to remove dirt and bacteria. Gently pat the area dry with a clean cloth. Apply an antiseptic ointment to prevent infection, then cover the wound with a sterile bandage. Change the bandage daily or whenever it becomes dirty or wet. Keeping the wound clean and covered helps it heal faster and reduces the risk of infection.

Burns are another common injury. It's good to think about the different types of burns and how they each require different treatment. First-degree burns affect only the outer layer of skin, causing redness and pain. Second-degree burns damage deeper layers and can result in blisters. Third-degree burns are the most severe, damaging all layers of the skin and possibly underlying tissues. For minor burns, immediately cool the area under running water for at least 10 minutes. This helps reduce pain and swelling. Avoid using ice or butter, as these can cause further damage. After cooling, cover the burn with a clean, non-stick bandage. If the burn is more severe or covers a large area, call the emergency services.

· · ·

Sprains and strains are common injuries, especially if into playing sports and heading down the gym now and then. Getting to grips with how to manage these injuries can prevent further damage and speed up recovery. The RICE method—Rest, Ice, Compression, Elevation—is a standard approach for treating sprains and strains. Rest the injured limb to prevent further strain. Apply ice to the area for 15-20 minutes every hour to reduce swelling. Use a compression bandage to support the injured area and minimize swelling. Finally, elevate the injured limb above heart level to reduce swelling and pain. Following these steps can significantly improve recovery time and reduce discomfort.

First Aid Kit Checklist

It's always good to be prepared. Let's think about our preparedness in terms of the materials and equipment we need to have to hand in case of an emergency.

Here's a checklist to get you started:

- Adhesive bandages in various sizes
- Sterile gauze pads
- Antiseptic wipes and ointment
- Tweezers and scissors
- Elastic bandages
- Thermometer
- Pain relievers (e.g., ibuprofen, acetaminophen)
- Disposable gloves
- Instant cold packs
- First aid manual

. . .

Having these items readily available can make a big difference when dealing with minor injuries.

Being prepared for emergencies involves more than just knowing how to react; it requires having the right tools and knowledge. Understanding the basics of first aid, treating cuts and scrapes, managing burns, and handling sprains and strains are all just things we have to know. By staying calm, assessing the situation, and knowing when to call for help, you can provide effective care and potentially save lives – but still, let's hope that it never comes to that.

5.2 CREATING AN EMERGENCY PLAN

Often, families take it upon themselves to design a 'Family Emergency Plan'. Such a plan ensures everyone knows what to do when disaster strikes, minimizing chaos and confusion. Start by discussing potential emergencies with your family – why not take some paper and mind-map together. Identify the types of disasters that could affect your area, such as fires, floods, or earthquakes. Each type of emergency requires a different response, so it's important to think about exactly what to do when if each were to arise. Sit down together and talk about what steps each person should take in various scenarios. This conversation helps everyone feel more prepared and less anxious about the unknown.

Designating a meeting place outside the home is an important part of your plan. Choose a location that's easy to find but a safe distance from your house, like a neighbor's yard or a nearby park.

This way, if your home becomes unsafe, everyone knows where to go to regroup. Make sure all family members are familiar with this spot. Assigning responsibilities to each family member can also streamline your emergency response. For example, one person could be in charge of grabbing the emergency kit, while another ensures all pets are safely evacuated. You could even have fun with it. Why not given names and characters to those roles – in this way, they can be fun for younger children, and often more memorable for everyone concerned.

Have you ever thought about who you would contact? Do you currently have a physical list of emergency contact? Ensure everyone in the family knows the local emergency numbers for the fire department, police, and ambulance services. Keep this list in an easily accessible place, like on the refrigerator or near the phone. Consider keeping contact information for close family members and friends in the same place. In an emergency, you may need to reach out to them for help or to let them know you're safe. Numbers for close neighbors can also be helpful, especially if you need immediate assistance or a place to stay temporarily.

What about making an emergency kit? This kit should include first aid supplies like bandages, antiseptics, and pain relievers. A flashlight with extra batteries is greatly needed for power outages. Make sure to have bottled water and non-perishable food items that can sustain your family for at least 72 hours. Key medications and medical supplies should also be included. If anyone in the family has specific medical needs, ensure those items are part of your kit, such as an EpiPen. Personal hygiene items, blankets, and multi-purpose tools can also be beneficial.

Store your kit in a portable container so it can be easily grabbed in an evacuation.

Regularly reviewing and updating your emergency plan ensures it remains effective, after all, things do change and we need to factor in those changes. As part of games night, or another occasion when you might all be together, go over the plan and make any necessary changes. Life changes, such as moving to a new house or a family member developing new health needs, can require updates to your plan. Make it a habit to review and update your emergency contact information and the contents of your emergency kit. Why not mark it in your calendar so it doesn't get put aside? You might want to consider practicing fire drills, as these and knowing evacuation routes, helps everyone remember what to do and makes the process more efficient. These drills can be especially helpful for younger children, who may need extra practice to feel comfortable with the plan.

Remember: incorporating these steps into your family's routine can greatly improve how you handle emergencies. Let's look at the key points:

- Discuss potential scenarios
- Designate a meeting place
- Assign responsibilities
- Keep an emergency kit ready
- Regularly review and keep it up to date

With a solid plan in place, you'll feel more confident and prepared to act quickly in unexpected situations.

5.3 HANDLING COMMON HOUSEHOLD EMERGENCIES

Home emergencies can happen fast, but knowing how to handle them can stop small problems from becoming big ones. Let's look at some common household emergencies and how to manage them efficiently.

Kitchen Fires

Dealing with such events is a critical life skill. If a fire starts while you're cooking, the first step is to stay calm and act quickly. Turn off the heat source immediately to prevent the fire from growing. Use a fire extinguisher if you have one. Make sure you know how to operate it beforehand: pull the pin, aim the nozzle at the base of the fire, squeeze the handle, and sweep from side to side. If you don't have a fire extinguisher, smother the flames with a lid if the fire is in a pan or use baking soda. Never use water on a grease fire —it can make the flames spread. Of course, if you think it cannot be contained via these steps, call the fire department.

Electrical Outages

Managing these involves a few key precautions to keep your home safe. Unplug sensitive electronics like computers and TVs to prevent damage from power surges when electricity finally gets restored. Use flashlights instead of candles to avoid fire hazards; keep a supply of batteries and monitor local news over the cellular network for information on the outage. It's also wise to have a stash of non-perishable food and bottled water, especially if the outage lasts for an extended period – of course, these can be the same as those you've already prepared for your emergency kit, as mentioned above. If you've done all this prep, if it happens, you can just sit back and enjoy a board game or two with the family until the power comes back on.

Water Leaks and Flooding

This is surely the nightmare of any homeowner! But act quickly, and everything should be fine. If you notice a leak, turn off the main water supply immediately to stop the flow of water. Use buckets, towels, or a wet/dry vacuum to contain and remove the water. Now, like a detective, we must hunt down the source of the leak. Sometimes, it might be a simple fix, like tightening a pipe, however, for significant leaks or if you're unsure, contact a plumber. Regularly checking for signs of leaks, such as damp spots on walls or ceilings, can help you catch problems early and prevent extensive damage later on. You may be interested to know that there now exist some fairly modern and intricate gadgets for the home; devices, for example, which automatically react to potential floods and cut the supply automatically. Speak to a local plumber if you're interested in such devices.

Gas Leaks

Time to act fast! This is a situation that requires you to think on your feet. If you ever smell gas, which often has a sulfur-like odor, evacuate the home immediately. Do not use electrical switches, lighters, or anything that could create a spark as this could ignite the gas and cause an explosion. Leave doors and windows open to allow the gas to dissipate if you can access them easily. Once you're at a safe distance, call the gas company and emergency services to report the leak. Do not re-enter the house until it has been declared safe by professionals. Familiarize yourself with how to shut off the gas supply in your home as a precautionary measure.

Handling common household emergencies can protect lives and property. Being prepared and knowing what to do can make a big difference. Stay safe and call for help when needed – this is the take home message.

5.4 STAYING SAFE DURING NATURAL DISASTERS

Natural disasters can strike without warning. But what might be the best way to prepare for such eventualities? Earthquake preparedness is one such thing we might have to think about depending on where we live. Securing heavy furniture and appliances is a good starting point if your area is prone to such disasters. Use brackets or straps to anchor bookshelves, dressers, and other large items to the walls. This prevents them from toppling over during an earthquake. Identifying safe spots – or areas where to shelter - in each room, such as under sturdy tables or desks, can provide immediate protection, close to hand. Practicing "Drop, Cover, and Hold On" drills with your family helps everyone know what to do if the ground starts to shake. Drop to your hands and knees, cover your head and neck with your arms, and hold on to something sturdy until the shaking stops.

· · ·

Tornadoes are another type of natural disaster that requires specific safety measures. Allocating a safe room or storm shelter in your home is a great way to start. This could be a basement, storm cellar, or an interior room on the lowest floor with no windows. Keeping a weather radio and an emergency kit in this safe room ensures you have access to essential information and supplies. Tornado warning signs, such as dark, greenish skies, large hail, and a loud roar similar to a freight train, should prompt you to take immediate action. Move to your designated safe room and stay there until the danger has passed.

Hurricane preparedness involves several steps to ensure your safety during the storm. Boarding up windows and securing outdoor items can prevent them from flying all over the place in high winds. If authorities issue an evacuation order, follow it promptly. Getting on top of this early helps you avoid the worst conditions and ensures you reach a safe location. Stocking up on essential supplies like food, water, and medications is crucial. Aim to have enough supplies to last at least three days. Again, think emergency kit.

Floods are common natural disasters, so it's important to know how to stay safe. Avoid walking or driving through floodwaters, as they can be deceptively dangerous. If a flood occurs, move to higher ground immediately! Just six inches of moving water can knock you off your feet, and a foot of water can sweep away a car. Listening to emergency broadcasts for updates and instructions ensures you have the latest information on what do to and where to go.

· · ·

So, you can see how just a few simple things can make a huge difference when it comes to being prepared for natural disasters. Securing your home, identifying safe spots, and practicing emergency drills make a big difference in how well you handle potential earthquakes, tornadoes, hurricanes, and floods. Staying informed and having a plan ensures you and your family can respond quickly and effectively when disaster strikes.

CHAPTER SIX

MENTAL HEALTH SUPPORT

In high school, it wasn't long for me before I felt the pressure of balancing everything; it was really like spinning plates – homework, schoolwork, extracurricular activities – the list goes on. In the midst of this, one day, I remember vividly sitting on the edge of my bed and realizing that my heart was pounding, like it was going to pop out of my chest. Suddenly I couldn't focus on anything. It would be many years later until I discovered that what I had experienced was a panic attack, induced because of stress. Let's dig deep in this chapter. Mental health is almost a pandemic nowadays, especially for younger people and so we owe it our utmost care and consideration.

6.1 RECOGNIZING AND MANAGING STRESS

As many specialists in this area would attest to, noticing and be aware of the signs of stress is not only the first step, but is some kind of ability we should constantly have switched on. Stress can manifest in various ways, and understanding these signs can help you take action before it becomes overwhelming. Physical symptoms of stress include headaches and muscle tension; have you ever felt tense in your jaw? It's most likely it is stress-related. If you find yourself frequently reaching for painkillers or noticing tightness in your body, the culprit is likely to be stress. Emotionally, stress can make you feel irritable or overwhelmed. Small problems might seem insurmountable, and you might find yourself snapping at friends or family over minor issues. Behavioral changes are also common. You might notice a shift in your sleep patterns, either struggling to fall asleep, waking up too early, or waking up frequently during the night. Withdrawal from activities you once enjoyed is another red flag, not only of stress but even of depression. If you're distancing yourself from social events or hobbies, it's time to take a closer look at what's going on.

Identifying triggers is one option to get on top of this. Academic pressures are a significant source of stress for many teens. Exams, homework, and the pressure to perform well can create constant tension. Social stressors, such as peer relationships and family dynamics, can also contribute. Arguments with friends, bullying, or strained relationships at home can add to your stress levels. Nowadays, unfortunately, many of these are made worse through the widespread use of smartphones and social media. But we shouldn't count out environmental factors too, like noise and clutter, which can exacerbate stress without you even realizing it. A noisy environment can make it hard to concentrate, while a cluttered space can make you feel more overwhelmed. Just noticing these triggers is a sure fire way to begin understanding how to combat them.

· · ·

Did you know that having some go-to stress management techniques can significantly improve your ability to cope with stress? Deep breathing exercises are a simple yet effective way to calm your mind and body. Try taking slow, deep breaths, inhaling through your nose and exhaling through your mouth. This can help lower your heart rate and reduce tension. Progressive muscle relaxation is another technique. It involves tensing and then relaxing different muscle groups in your body, helping you release physical tension. Often people start with their temples and then work their way down the entire body until they reach the toes.

Engaging in hobbies and activities that you enjoy can also be a great way to let off steam and de-stress. Whether it's painting, playing a sport, or listening to music, doing something you love can provide a much-needed mental break. Time management strategies can also help you reduce stress. By organizing your tasks and setting realistic deadlines, you can avoid the last-minute rush and feel more in control (see earlier chapters on effective time management to assist here).

Like with so many things, a plan can be a good way to stay on top of your game and combat stress. Start by identifying your specific stressors and the coping mechanisms that work best for you. For instance, if academic pressure is a major stressor, you might find that setting aside dedicated study times and breaking down assignments into smaller tasks helps. Setting realistic goals and priorities is crucial. It's easy to feel overwhelmed when you're trying to do too much at once. Break your tasks into manageable chunks and prioritize what's most important. Incorporating regular relaxation practices into your routine can also make a big difference. This might include activities like those mentioned above, or, if you have more time available, yoga, meditation, or simply taking a walk outside. Seeking support from friends, family, or counselors is another important component. Talking about your stress and getting advice from others can provide new perspectives and help you feel less alone. At the end of the day, we are all human and we all suffer from stress from time to time.

Stress Management Plan Template

Here is a simple plan for you to use; it's designed to be adaptable and can be easily personalized. The idea is that such planning can help you in the short-term and the long-term, as you learn more about your triggers and how to sidestep them.

1. **Identify Your Stressors:**
   - Academic pressures
   - Social stressors
   - Environmental factors
2. **Coping Mechanisms:**
   - Deep breathing exercises
   - Progressive muscle relaxation
   - Engaging in hobbies and activities
3. **Setting Realistic Goals and Priorities:**
   - Break tasks into smaller, manageable parts
   - Prioritize what's most important
4. **Incorporate Relaxation Practices:**
   - Yoga or meditation
   - Walks outside
   - Listening to music

5. **Seek Support:**
   - Talk to friends and family
   - Consult a school counselor

Stress is a part of life, but with the right tools and strategies, you can handle it effectively and keep it from taking over. So why not give the template a go?

6.2 TECHNIQUES FOR ANXIETY RELIEF

Unlike normal stress, which is a response to specific situations, anxiety often feels more pervasive and persistent. Physical symptoms of anxiety can include a racing heart and sweating. You might notice your heart pounding as if you've just run a marathon or feel drenched in sweat even in a cool room. Cognitive symptoms are equally challenging. Excessive worrying and intrusive thoughts can make it hard to focus on anything else. You may find yourself constantly thinking about worst-case scenarios or replaying stressful events in your mind. Behavioral symptoms often manifest as avoidance and irritability. You might start avoiding social situations or activities that trigger your anxiety. Restlessness, or feeling irritable, can make it hard to sit still, leading to constant fidgeting or pacing.

Practicing mindfulness and meditation can be incredibly effective in reducing anxiety. These scientifically-proven techniques can help you stay grounded in the present moment, making it easier to manage anxious thoughts and feelings. Most, if not all, use the principle of refocusing your attention – often to your breath or to a part of your body. Guided meditation exercises can be a good starting point. These exercises often involve listening to a recorded voice that guides you through the process of focusing your mind and relaxing your body. Mindful breathing techniques are another powerful tool. Try focusing on your breath, taking slow, deep inhales through your nose and exhaling through your mouth. This simple act can help calm your mind and body. Body scan meditation involves paying attention to different parts of your body, from your toes to your head, noticing any sensations without judgment. This practice can help you become more aware of how anxiety affects your body and mind. None of these techniques are particularly easy at first, but with time, they can become second nature. You don't have to go it alone; there are a bunch of apps and YouTube videos made specifically to guide you through. Often, after some months, you no longer need to rely on them, and you can navigate your own system – one that is better suited to you as an individual.

Cognitive-behavioral techniques (CBT) offer practical ways to manage anxiety by changing how you think and behave. One effective CBT method is identifying and challenging negative thoughts. When you notice a negative thought, ask yourself if it's based on facts or assumptions. Reframe it into a more balanced perspective. For example, if you think, "I'm going to fail this test," challenge that thought by considering your preparation and past successes. Developing positive affirmations can also help. Create statements that counteract negative beliefs, such as "I am capable and prepared." Practicing exposure therapy for phobias involves gradually facing the situations or objects you fear in a controlled and safe manner. Over time, this can help reduce the fear and anxiety associated with those situations. Although there are some tools online or in some specialized apps, people tend to seek professional advice from a psychologist when it comes to the techniques mentioned above.

Lifestyle changes can also play a significant role in reducing anxiety levels. Regular physical exercise is one of the most effective ways to manage anxiety. Activities like jogging, swimming, or even walking can release endorphins, which are natural mood lifters. It goes without saying that maintaining a balanced diet is equally important. Eating a variety of nutrient-rich foods can help keep your energy levels stable and your mind sharp. Alongside this, is getting enough sleep. This is crucial for good mental health. Aim for 7-9 hours of quality sleep each night. A consistent sleep schedule can help regulate your body's internal clock, making it easier to fall asleep and wake up. Limiting caffeine and sugar intake can also make a big difference. Both can cause spikes and crashes in energy levels, leading to worse anxiety symptoms. Again, if sleep is a huge problem, don't feel shy about speaking to your family doctor.

Making these changes might seem overwhelming at first, but small steps can lead to significant improvements – overall, it comes down to identifying what the issue is primarily, then thinking about, working with others, to develop solutions to what are essentially symptoms, just like having a runny nose. Many benefit though from introducing mindfulness practices into their daily routine, even if it's just for a few minutes each day. Try a short guided meditation before bed or practice mindful breathing during a break at school or at work. Use cognitive-behavioral techniques to challenge negative thoughts as they arise and develop positive affirmations to reinforce your strengths. Incorporate physical exercise into your week, whether it's a morning jog or an evening yoga session. Pay attention to your diet and sleep habits, making adjustments as needed to support your mental well-being. To sum up, what is often misunderstood is that these techniques are like a plaster, that you only put on when you've cut yourself; this is not the case. These things are preventative, like wearing a helmet. For this reason, they often need to be done over a long period of time to reap the rewards.

6.3 BUILDING EMOTIONAL RESILIENCE

Life is full of ups and downs. The shift from one to the other very often has little to do with our actions. Emotional resilience is your ability to bounce back from setbacks and adapt to challenging circumstances – i.e. to handle the shifts. It's about developing a positive outlook and building strong support networks that can help you through tough times. Imagine it as a rubber band: when stretched, it returns to its original shape. The same goes for your emotional well-being. With resilience, you can recover more quickly from difficulties and continue moving forward.

Strengthening emotional resilience involves several strategies. Developing problem-solving skills comes first on our list. As before, when we talked about managing our time effectively, when faced with a challenge, break it down into smaller, manageable parts. This makes the problem seem less scary and allows you to tackle it step by step. Practicing gratitude and positive thinking can also make a significant difference. Start by keeping a gratitude journal where you jot down things you're thankful for each day. This practice shifts your focus from what's wrong to what's right in your life. Engaging in regular self-reflection and journaling helps you understand your emotions and reactions. Take time to write about your experiences, how they made you feel at the time, and what you learned from them. This not only provides an emotional outlet but also helps you gain insights into your coping mechanisms.

Building healthy relationships plays a vital role in supporting the emotions too. Being able to talk easily with friends and family is the cornerstone of strong relationships. Be open about your feelings and listen actively when others share theirs. This mutual understanding fosters trust and support. Setting and respecting boundaries is key. Know your limits and communicate them clearly to others, ensuring that your relationships are balanced and healthy. Seeking out supportive and positive individuals can provide the encouragement and perspective you need during challenging times. Surround yourself with people who uplift you and contribute to your growth. It's sometimes hard to identify a toxic person, but it is a necessary evil as we try to develop connections that give, and not take.

Having what is often called a growth-mindset can lead to many positive changes. It boils down to seeing challenges as opportunities for growth rather than obstacles you can't climb over. When faced with a setback, remind yourself that it's a chance to learn and improve. Try to think about exactly what a mistake is. It should really be a chance to learn, not something that we should mull over for days. Instead of dwelling on failures, analyze what went wrong and how you can do better next time. This approach helps you develop a more positive and proactive attitude towards challenges.

. . .

Daily Gratitude Journal

As mentioned, keeping a gratitude journal can help you focus on the positive aspects of your life, helping you to feel more positive.

Here's a simple way to get started:

1. **Morning Reflection:**
   - What are three things you're looking forward to today?
   - How can you make today a good day for yourself and others?
2. **Evening Reflection:**
   - What are three things you're grateful for that happened today?
   - What is one thing you learned today, and how can it help you in the future?

Again, it might not be something you adapt to quickly, but it's worth giving it a go and see how you feel. It's about reframing ideas so you can always stay on top of the game, and not let negativity drag you down.

6.4 SEEKING PROFESSIONAL HELP AND SUPPORT

As mentioned in previous sections; it's not always necessary or advised to go it alone for everything. Sometimes, the signs are clear, like persistent feelings of sadness or hopelessness that just won't go away. If you find it hard to get out of bed, lose interest in activities you once loved, or feel like you're carrying a heavy emotional weight, it's time to take action. Difficulty functioning in daily life is another red flag. If tasks that used to be easy, like going to school, hanging out with friends, or even eating and sleeping, become overwhelming, professional support can help you get back on track. In more severe cases, thoughts of self-harm or suicide need immediate attention; if these thoughts cross your mind, reach out to a trusted adult or mental health professional right away. You don't have to face this alone, and there are many people and organizations ready and willing to help.

There are many different types of Mental Healthcare Professionals, each offering unique services to support your mental health. Psychologists specialize in assessing and treating mental health issues through therapy. They can help you understand your thoughts, feelings, and behaviors and work with you to develop coping strategies. Psychiatrists are medical doctors who can diagnose mental health conditions and prescribe medication if needed. They often work alongside therapists to provide the best possible care. Counselors and therapists offer a safe space to talk about your concerns and provide guidance on how to manage them. They use various therapeutic techniques to help you navigate life's challenges. School counselors are another valuable resource. They are trained to help students deal with academic and personal issues and can provide support and referrals if you need more specialized care.

Finding a therapist or counselor can start with a simple search online. Websites like Psychology Today offer directories of mental health professionals, including their specialties, locations, and contact information. Utilizing school and community resources can also be beneficial. Many schools have counseling services, and community centers often offer mental health programs. Online mental health services and hotlines provide immediate support and can be a good starting point if you're unsure where to turn. Services like BetterHelp and Talkspace connect you with licensed therapists through virtual sessions, making it easier to get help from the comfort of your home.

Talk openly about your experiences and listen without judgment when others share theirs. Sharing personal stories of seeking help can also be powerful and, overall, it can reduce the stigma that mental health often carries. When you hear about others who have faced similar struggles and found support, it can make you feel less isolated and more hopeful. Encouraging open communication with trusted individuals, whether friends, family members, or teachers, creates a supportive network where you feel safe to express your feelings and seek advice.

Here's a simple resource list to help you start your mental health journey:

1. **Online Directories:**
   - Psychology Today
   - GoodTherapy
2. **Online Therapy Services:**
   - BetterHelp
   - Talkspace

3. **Hotlines:**
   - National Suicide Prevention Lifeline: 1-800-273-8255
   - Crisis Text Line: Text HOME to 741741
4. **School and Community Resources:**
   - School counseling services
   - Local community centers
5. **Support Groups:**
   - National Alliance on Mental Illness (NAMI)
   - Mental Health America (MHA)

Remember: although not always necessary, professional help is sometimes inevitable. Recognizing when you need help, understanding the types of mental health professionals, accessing resources, and overcoming stigma are all steps towards a healthier, more balanced life. By taking these steps, you can ensure that you're not alone in facing your challenges and have the support needed to thrive.

In the next chapter, we will explore the importance of social skills and building relationships, things which are deeply connected to having good mental health. We'll pay special attention to how they contribute to your overall well-being and success.

CHAPTER SEVEN

THE DEVELOPMENT OF SOCIAL SKILLS

I'll admit it – I was painfully shy. But that's okay. Perhaps we all are at some points in our lives. Even the confident kids surely get the jitters before a performance or a presentation in front of the class. This was my particular pet-peeve in fact. I would worry for weeks, imagining everything that would go wrong – not might; I knew it was going to be a disaster. Over time, and because of such thoughts, it was necessary for me to develop a new attitude; one which focused on the positives. Let's zero in on this and discuss the vital importance of effective communication as a key life skill. After all, social skills like this are not just about talking; they're about connecting, understanding, and influencing others. This chapter will guide you through mastering these skills, setting you up for success in both personal and professional settings.

7.1 EFFECTIVE COMMUNICATION SKILLS

Effective communication is the foundation of all relationships. It's how we convey our ideas, emotions, and needs. Verbal communication involves the words we choose, but non-verbal communication often conveys a lot more. Body language, facial expressions, and posture all send powerful messages. For instance, crossing your arms can signal defensiveness, while maintaining an open stance shows you are approachable. Facial expressions convey emotions; a smile can make you seem friendly, while a frown might suggest annoyance. Tone and pitch in verbal communication also play significant roles. A calm, steady tone can convey confidence, while a high-pitched, hurried tone might indicate nervousness. Whilst often these things happen without us being aware, we can become aware of such things, and make efforts to adjust them to aid in how we communicate effectively.

Being able to actively listen is what we all want from others, so why not ensure that we too have this important skill. It's not just about hearing the words but understanding the message behind them – reading in between the lines. Making eye contact shows the speaker you are engaged. Nodding and using affirming gestures like "uh-huh" or "I see" can encourage them to continue. Reflecting back what the speaker said demonstrates you are listening and understanding. For example, if a friend says, "I had a tough day at school," you might respond, "It sounds like your day was really challenging." Asking clarifying questions can also help deepen the conversation. Questions like, "Can you tell me more about that?" or "What happened next?" show genuine interest and encourage the speaker to open up.

Being assertive is about expressing your thoughts and feelings honestly while respecting others. There are different communication styles: passive, aggressive, passive-aggressive, and assertive.

Passive communicators avoid conflict and suppress their feelings, often leading to frustration. Aggressive communicators prioritize their own needs without considering others, which can create tension. Passive-aggressive communicators use sarcasm or the silent treatment instead of addressing issues directly. Assertive communication, on the other hand, involves being honest and direct while respecting others' opinions and feelings. Using "I" statements is a key part of assertive communication. Instead of saying, "You never listen to me," which can sound like you are blaming the other person, try saying, "I don't feel listened to when you interrupt me." This approach focuses on your feelings and reduces the likelihood of the other person becoming defensive.

Setting and respecting boundaries is another aspect of assertive communication. For example, if a friend constantly borrows your things without asking, you might say, "I need you to ask before borrowing my stuff." This sets a clear expectation without being confrontational. Assertive communication can be applied in various scenarios, whether it's speaking up in class, discussing responsibilities at home, or negotiating tasks at work. It's about finding a balance between your needs and others', fostering mutual respect and understanding.

Public speaking is an essential skill that goes hand in hand with effective communication. Whether you're presenting in class, leading a team meeting, or speaking at an event, strong public speaking skills can set you apart. Preparing and organizing your content is the first step. Know your material well, and structure your presentation with a clear beginning, middle, and end. Practicing your delivery is equally important. Rehearse in front of a mirror, record yourself, or practice with friends to get feedback. Pay attention to your body language; stand tall, make eye contact, and use hand gestures to emphasize points. Managing public speaking anxiety is a common challenge. Deep breathing exercises can help calm your nerves before you get up to talk. Remember, it's okay to pause and collect your thoughts if you lose your place. Engaging the audience can make your presentation more interactive and less intimidating. Ask questions, invite participation, or use visual aids to keep the audience interested.

7.2 PUBLIC SPEAKING PRACTICE

Take a topic you're passionate about and prepare a 3-minute presentation. Practice delivering it in front of a mirror or record yourself. Pay attention to your body language, tone, and pacing. As you watch back, reflect on areas for improvement and practice again. Don't forget to jot down what was good too – and make sure to keep this up the next time. Why not do this often? You'll find that, as you become conscious of your delivery, you'll increase in confidence and ability.

Improving your communication skills can truly enhance your connections and relationships. Whether it's picking up on body language, listening attentively, speaking with confidence, or simply getting better at public speaking, these abilities can help you engage with others in a more genuine way. By mastering them, you'll find it easier to navigate different social situations with ease and build stronger, more meaningful interactions.

7.3 BUILDING HEALTHY FRIENDSHIPS

Healthy friendships form a vital part of your social world, and knowing what to look for in a friend can make all the difference. We mentioned previously too that forming these can help us combat the mental health storms we might be faced with. Let's start with trust; a good friend is someone you can rely on to keep your secrets and support you through thick and thin. Without trust, a friendship lacks a solid foundation. Empathy and understanding are equally important. A friend who listens and tries to understand your feelings can offer true comfort and support. They don't just hear your words; they feel your emotions. Reliability is another key trait. Friends who show up when they say they will and follow through on promises build a sense of security in the relationship. Shared interests and values often bring people together, creating a natural bond. Whether it's a love for the same sports team, hobby, or even shared moral values, these 'things in common' can help strengthen the bond.

Making new friends might not always seem easy, but the rewards you'll get far outweigh the effort you put in. Joining clubs or extracurricular activities is a fantastic way to meet people with similar interests. Whether it's a sports team, drama club, or a debate society, these settings provide a common ground for interaction. Volunteering for community service also opens doors to new friendships. Working together towards a common goal is a sure-fire way to build connections and find ways to respect others. Starting conversations with people your same age in class or at events can be as simple as commenting on shared experiences or interests. A compliment or a question about a class you both share can be a great way to break the ice. Social media, when used responsibly, can also be a tool for making new friends. Plat-forms like Instagram or Twitter allow you to connect with peers, share interests, and even arrange meetups. However, it's crucial to use these platforms wisely and ensure your online interactions are safe and respectful.

Maintaining friendships requires effort and commitment, but it is at the heart of what it means to live a fulfilling existence. After all, communication is the lifeblood of any friendship. Whether it's a quick text, a call, or face-to-face meetings, staying in touch helps keep the bond strong. Show appreciation and gratitude to your friends by acknowledging their efforts and expressing thanks. A simple "thank you" can go a long way in making someone feel valued. Being supportive during tough times is another crucial aspect. Life can be challenging, and having a friend who stands by you during difficult moments can make all the difference.

We're all going to face challenges when it comes to keeping a friendship strong, but knowing how to address these issues can save the relationship. Jealousy or competition can strain a friend-ship, for example. If you feel these emotions creeping in, address them openly and honestly. Discussing your feelings can help clear misunderstandings and strengthen your bond. These, as well as other kinds of miscommunications will always happen, but they don't have to end friendships. Clarify your intentions, listen to your friend's point of view, and find a resolution together. Balancing multiple friendships can sometimes be tricky, but it's doable with good time management and clear communication. Make time for each friend and ensure no one feels neglected. As mentioned previously, when we discussed emotional resilience, when to end a toxic friendship is also essential. If a friend consistently disrespects you, breaks your trust, or negatively impacts your well-being, it might be time to reconsider the relationship.

Friendship is a journey filled with ups and downs, but understanding these dynamics can help you build and maintain meaningful relationships.

7.4 NAVIGATING ROMANTIC RELATIONSHIPS

Understanding what makes a romantic relationship tick can be the key to both happiness and emotional well-being. Let's state first off that the heart of a strong relationship is mutual respect. This means valuing each other's opinions, feelings, and boundaries. Respect is about seeing your partner as an equal and treating them with kindness and consideration. Open and honest communication is another pillar. This involves sharing your thoughts and feelings openly and listening to your partner without judgment. When you communicate honestly, misunderstandings are less likely to occur, and trust is built over time.

Shared values and interests also form the core of many successful relationships. While it's not necessary to agree on everything, having common ground in key areas like future goals, lifestyle choices, and moral beliefs can strengthen your bond. Enjoying similar activities or hobbies can also provide opportunities to spend quality time together. Support and encouragement from your partner can make facing life's challenges more manageable. Whether it's cheering you on during a school project or comforting you after a tough day, knowing that someone has your back can be incredibly reassuring. But this is a two-way street, and often in relationships you get what you give.

Attraction is often important in the initial stages, but most of us soon realize that it is even more important to get to know the person. Spend time talking about your dreams, fears, and experiences. Understanding your partner's background and views on life and love can deepen your connection. Setting boundaries and expectations early on can prevent misunderstandings. Discuss what you're comfortable with and what you expect from each other in terms of time, affection, and communication. Building trust is a gradual process. It involves being reliable, keeping promises, and showing that you can be counted on. Trust can be fragile, so handling it with care is vital.

All relationships going through rough patches. It's something we have to live with, more importantly, know how to live through and reach effective solutions. Good communication during disagreements is key. Instead of letting emotions ride high, take a moment to breathe and then discuss the issue calmly. Use "I" statements to express your feelings without blaming your partner. You might want to even consider the time you spend apart from each other. While it's great to spend time together, maintaining your individual interests and friendships keeps the relationship healthy. Handling jealousy and insecurity requires addressing your feelings openly. Talk to your partner about what triggers these emotions and work together to build reassurance. Recognizing and addressing red flags in a relationship is crucial. If you notice patterns of disrespect, dishonesty, or controlling behavior, it's important to address these issues early on and decide if the relationship is healthy for you.

Maintaining intimacy and connection in a romantic relationship requires ongoing effort. Regularly spending quality time together helps keep the bond strong. Whether it's a weekly date night or simply watching a movie together, these moments of connection are important. Expressing love and appreciation can be done in many ways, from saying "I love you" to small gestures like leaving a sweet note or doing something thoughtful. Always keep an open channel to each other, so you both know that you can contact the other if either person needs a little pick-me-up. Most importantly though, get out there, do shared activities and hobbies to create new memories and strengthen your connection.

In a romantic relationship, maintaining a strong and fulfilling connection comes down to a few key principles. Let's summarize what we've spoken about so far:

- Navigate challenges together with open communication and understanding.
- Build a solid foundation of trust and respect.
- Foster intimacy through shared experiences and emotional closeness.
- Address common issues with patience, empathy, and proactive solutions.

With these strategies, you can create a partnership that thrives on mutual support and long-term happiness.

7.5 CONFLICT RESOLUTION AND NEGOTIATION

Look, we can't all be best buds, 100% of the time. Sometimes conflicts will crop up and it's true that they can arise for various reasons. Misunderstandings and miscommunications are common culprits. A simple misinterpretation of someone's words or actions can escalate into a full-blown conflict if not addressed in a timely fashion. Differences in values and beliefs also play a significant role. For instance, one person might prioritize family time, while another values burning the midnight oil and working towards that promotion. These differing priorities can lead to disagreements. Competition for resources or attention is another source of conflict. In a school setting, students might compete for the teacher's attention or for limited resources like books and computers. Personality clashes can also spark conflicts. People have different temperaments and ways of handling situations, and these differences can sometimes lead to friction. Let's look at some of these things in more detail so we can get to grips with resolving our conflicts in a more satisfying way.

First off, like so many things, a structured approach is needed. The first step is identifying the root cause of the conflict. Understanding why the conflict arose helps in addressing the real issue rather than just the symptoms. As mentioned in several sections already, using "I" statements to express feelings and perspectives is encouraged. Finding common ground and mutual interests can also help. Look for areas where both parties agree, even if it's something small. This can serve as a foundation for resolving the larger issue. Developing a plan for resolution involves brainstorming solutions together. Both parties should have a say in the final decision, ensuring that the solution is acceptable to everyone involved. Think of it as a democratic process! After all is said and done, we all want our voices to be heard.

Negotiation skills are invaluable when it comes to resolving conflicts and reaching mutually beneficial agreements. It's best to start with a bit of prep-work. Research the issue thoroughly and set clear goals for what you want to achieve. Knowing your priorities and limits helps you stay focused during the negotiation. Listening actively to the other party's perspective is equally important. This involves not just hearing their words but understanding their concerns and motivations. Proposing solutions and compromises is the next step. Aim for win-win solutions that address both parties' needs. Finally, closing the negotiation with clear agreements ensures that everyone knows what has been decided. Alternatively, and in the hope of not creating an all-out war, think how you can be open. Think carefully, for example, about the words of Henry Kissinger, "A compromise is when both parties are dissatisfied." Jotting down key info concerning what has been decided can avoid the arguments from flaring up again in the future. As they say, "The pen is mightier than the sword."

Sometimes, conflicts cannot be resolved through negotiation alone. In these cases, seeking mediation or third-party assistance can be helpful. A neutral party can be brought in to set out a framework for both sides. Knowing when to walk away from a conflict is also important. If the conflict becomes too toxic or unresolvable, it might be best to disengage. Reflecting on the conflict to learn and grow is a great follow-up step. Analyze what went wrong and what could have been handled differently. This helps you handle future conflicts more effectively. Maintaining professionalism and respect despite disagreements is essential. Even if you don't agree with the other party, treating them with respect can prevent the conflict from escalating further.

In this chapter, we explored key elements that contribute to both personal and relationship success. From having effective communication and public speaking skills to building strong and healthy relationships, these abilities form the foundation for meaningful connections. By mastering conflict resolution and negotiation, we can navigate challenges with greater ease and understanding, ensuring a more harmonious and fulfilling life both personally and with those around us.

CHAPTER EIGHT

CAREER READINESS

I remember it well. I was a junior in high school. Career day had always seemed like quite an unusual event – like, why would I be giving any thought to what career I was going to do. I'm sure I wasn't even aware of half of the possibilities which are out there. I was wandering kind of aimlessly that day, not really listening properly to any of the presentations until I stumbled upon a talk from a psychologist. I was in awe – hooked from the first word. It was the first time I felt a real spark, a genuine interest in a particular profession. This is all it takes sometimes – a spark. This chapter is designed to guide you in exploring your career options, identifying your strengths, and setting goals that will help you achieve your dreams. Think of me as your Career Counselor for the next few pages!

8.1 EXPLORING CAREER OPTIONS

Identifying your interests and strengths is the first step in choosing a career that aligns with your passions and skills. Self-assessment tools can be incredibly helpful in this process. Tools like the O*NET Interest Profiler (https://www.onetcenter.org/tool s.html) allow you to answer questions about your likes and dislikes, which then suggests careers that might be a good fit for you. Reflect on your favorite subjects and hobbies. For instance, if you love solving math problems, engineering might be a good fit. If you enjoy writing, perhaps journalism or content creation is your calling. Seeking feedback from teachers, mentors, and family members can also provide valuable insights. They might notice strengths and talents you hadn't considered, offering a broader perspective on your capabilities.

Once you have a general idea of your interests, researching different careers can offer fresh perspectives and can give you a sense of what might be involved. Online career exploration tools like the Bureau of Labor Statistics' Occupational Outlook Handbook provide detailed information about various professions, including job responsibilities, required education, and salary expectations. Reading job descriptions and industry trends can also give you a sense of what skills are in demand and what a typical day in a particular career might look like. Why not reach out to people already in those fields? Send a simple email and ask them for information – straight from the horse's mouth, so to speak. Ask them about their job, the challenges they face, and what they enjoy most. This firsthand information can be invaluable in making an informed decision.

Understanding the educational and training requirements for different careers is something to get your head around early so you can better plan. Some careers require a college degree, while others might need vocational training or certifications. For example, becoming a doctor requires extensive education and training, including a bachelor's degree, medical school, and residency. On the other hand, careers in trades like plumbing or electrical work often require vocational training and apprenticeships. Exploring apprenticeship and internship opportunities can provide hands-on experience and a clearer understanding of the field. Continuous learning and professional development are essential regardless of the career you choose. Many professions require ongoing education to stay up-to-date with changes in your industry and to get those much-prized certificates.

Setting career goals based on your interests and research helps create a clear path forward. Start by setting short-term goals that are achievable within a few months to a year. These could include gaining relevant experience through internships, completing specific coursework, or developing a particular skill. Let's take an example. If you're interested in graphic design, a short-term goal might be to complete an online course in Adobe Photoshop. Long-term goals require more planning and might take several years to achieve. These could include obtaining a specific job title, advancing in your career, or starting your own business. Creating a career action plan with clear steps and deadlines can help you stay focused and motivated. Outline the steps needed to achieve your goals, such as the education required, skills to develop, and networking opportunities to pursue. Having a plan makes the process less overwhelming and provides a roadmap to follow.

To make this process more engaging, I've included a career exploration exercise. Take a moment to list three careers you're interested in. Use the tools I've already mentioned, like O*NET and the Bureau of Labor Statistics, to research these careers. Note down the required education, skills, and typical job responsibilities for each. Then, reflect on how your interests and strengths align with these careers. With so much choice out there, it's often a process of narrowing down to begin with, before you finally find your niche.

Exploring career options is a journey of self-discovery. By identifying your interests and strengths, researching different careers, understanding the educational requirements, and setting achievable goals, you can pave the way for a fulfilling professional life. Let's continue through the chapter and get equipped with the knowledge and tools to make life-changing decisions about our careers.

8.2 WRITING A COMPELLING RESUME

A resume is your mouthpiece – your first interaction with your future employer. Words can't really describe how useful it is and a powerful way to get your foot in the door. A resume serves as a marketing tool for job seekers, highlighting your skills and experiences to make a positive first impression on potential employers. It's essentially your professional story, condensed into one or two pages. Employers use resumes to quickly see if you're a good fit for the role. It's your chance to stand out from other applicants and showcase what you bring to the table. A well-crafted resume can lead you directly to interviews, and then jobs.

It's important to ensure that it's clear, concise, and professional. Start with your contact information at the top. This includes your name, phone number, email address, and sometimes your city and state. Make sure your email address is professional; something like yourname@gmail.com works best. Next, include an objective or summary statement. This brief section should outline your career goals and what you hope to achieve in the role. It's a snapshot of your ambitions and how they align with the job you're applying for.

Following that, you should list your education and relevant coursework. Include the name of your school, your expected graduation date, and any notable achievements or honors. If you've taken courses that are particularly relevant to the job, such as a coding class for a tech position, highlight those. Then, move on to work experience and internships. Even if you've only had part-time jobs or volunteer positions, list them. Focus on what you did and what you learned. Use bullet points to make this section easy to read. Finally, include a section for skills and certifications. Highlight both hard skills (like proficiency in software) and soft skills (like communication or teamwork).

To make your resume stand out, you need to effectively show your achievements and skills. Use action verbs to describe your responsibilities and accomplishments. Words like "managed," "developed," or "led" convey a sense of initiative and responsibility. For example, instead of saying "Responsible for social media," say "Managed social media accounts; increasing engagement by 20%." Quantifying achievements with specific metrics makes your contributions clear and impactful. Employers love to see numbers because they provide concrete evidence of your abilities. Highlight transferable skills that are relevant to the job. Skills like communication, teamwork, and problem-solving are valuable in almost any role. If you were part of a team project in school, mention how you collaborated to achieve a common goal.

It's best to develop your resume based on the job you are going for. A generic resume won't capture the specific qualifications employers are looking for. Start by analyzing the job posting to identify key qualifications and skills mentioned. Customize your objective statement and skills section to align with these requirements. For instance, if a job posting emphasizes the need for strong organizational skills, make sure to highlight your experience in managing projects or events. Including relevant keywords from the job description can help your resume pass through applicant tracking systems (ATS) that many companies use nowadays. These systems scan resumes for specific terms, and using the right keywords increases the chances of your resume being picked up by what will eventually be a human recruiter.

Resume Checklist

Here's a quick checklist to ensure your resume is ready for submission:

- Contact Information: Name, phone number, professional email address, city, and state.
- Objective/Summary Statement: Briefly outline your career goals and how they align with the job.
- Education: School name, expected graduation date, relevant courses, and achievements.

- Work Experience: Job titles, company names, dates of employment, and bullet points detailing responsibilities and accomplishments.
- Skills and Certifications: List both hard and soft skills as well as any relevant certifications.
- Action Verbs: Use strong action verbs to describe your roles ("completed", "brought about a change," "developed.")
- Metrics: Quantify achievements where possible.
- Keywords: Include keywords from the job description to pass the ATS.

Crafting a compelling resume requires attention to detail and a customized approach, but it's well within your grasp – just have patience. Understanding its purpose, structuring it properly, showcasing your skills effectively, and tailoring it to the job can make a significant difference in your job search.

8.3 ACING JOB INTERVIEWS

There's no two ways about it, job interviews need preparing for. But have fun with it – know that the effort you're putting in now is setting you up for life. Start by researching the company and its culture. Visit the company's website and read their mission statement, recent news articles, and any available employee testimonials. Understanding the company's values and work environment helps you match your responses to align with their expectations. Next, review the job description and requirements thoroughly. Highlight the key responsibilities and qualifications, and think about how your skills and experiences suit the position. Practicing common interview questions and answers is another crucial step. Questions like, "Tell me about yourself," "Why do you want to work here?" and "Describe a challenge you've faced and how you handled it" are common in many interviews. Practicing your answers helps you articulate your thoughts clearly and confidently. Lists of these questions can be easily found online, or, alternatively, there are many YouTube videos which provide wonderful instruction.

Dress to kill! Your clothing can significantly impact the first impression you make. Start by understanding the company's dress code. If the company culture leans towards business formal, go for a suit and tie or a professional dress. For a business casual environment, wear slacks or a skirt paired with a button-down shirt or blouse. Choose professional and comfortable clothing that fits well and makes you feel confident. Grooming and personal hygiene are also critical. Apart from the clothes, think about getting a haircut, trimming your beard (if you have one), and don't forget to brush your teeth – no one likes smelly breath.

The *STAR* method (Situation, Task, Action, and Result) is a proven way to answer behavioral questions effectively during the interview process. When asked to describe a past experience, start by outlining the situation, and then explain the task you were responsible for. Describe the action you took to address the task, and finish with the result of your efforts. For example, if asked about a time you led a project, you might say, "In my biology class (Situation), I was tasked with leading a group project on ecosystems (Task). I organized weekly meetings and delegated tasks based on each member's strengths (Action), resulting in a project that received an A and praise from our teacher (Result)." Along with what you say, be aware of the signs you're constantly giving off through your body. Maintain eye contact to show confidence and interest, offer a firm handshake, and sit up straight to convey professionalism. Asking insightful questions about the role and company shows your genuine interest and helps you gather valuable information. Questions like, "Can you describe a typical day in this role?" or "What are the biggest challenges facing the team right now?" can provide deeper insights into the job and demonstrate your enthusiasm.

Following up after the interview is a step that many overlook, but it can further show your interest in the position and leave a lasting impression. Send a thank-you email within 24 hours of the interview. Express your appreciation for the chance they've given you and mention specific points from the conversation that resonated with you. Personalizing the message makes it more memorable and shows that you were actively engaged during the interview. For example, you could say, "Thank you for taking the time to discuss the marketing intern position with me. I particularly enjoyed learning about the team's collaborative approach to project management." Expressing enthusiasm for the role and company demonstrates your interest and leaves a positive impression. Conclude with a statement like, "I am very excited about the possibility of joining your team and contributing to the innovative projects."

Getting ready for a job interview is simple enough really. It means doing the research, dressing right, learning a few key tips and sending a personal thank-you note afterward. These steps can help you feel confident, leave a good impression, and boost your chances of getting the job. Good luck!

8.4 BUILDING A PROFESSIONAL NETWORK

Networking can often seem like just a buzzword, but it's popularity should make you think twice about it's true importance. Building relationships with professionals in your industry can open doors, allowing you to explore a number of different options. By connecting with experienced individuals, you gain insights and advice that can be invaluable as you navigate your career path. These relationships can also give you access to the hidden job market through referrals. Many job openings aren't advertised publicly; they are filled through word-of-mouth and personal recommendations. Having a strong network increases your chances of being considered for these opportunities.

Building your professional network can feel overwhelming at first, but with a few practical strategies, it can become easier and even fun. Attending career fairs and industry events is a great way to meet professionals in your field. These events provide a platform to learn about different companies, ask questions, and make connections. Joining professional organizations and clubs related to your career interests can also be a great step forward. These groups often host events, workshops, and networking opportunities that allow you to meet like-minded individuals. Utilizing social media platforms like LinkedIn is another effective strategy. LinkedIn allows you to connect with professionals, join industry groups, and participate in discussions. Volunteering for community service or internships not only provides valuable experience but also helps you meet people who can become part of your professional network.

Maintaining and expanding your network over time is just as important as laying the foundations. Regularly keeping in touch with your contacts can help maintain these relationships. This doesn't mean bombarding them with messages but rather checking in every once in a while to see how they are doing and updating them on your progress. Offering help and support to others in your network can strengthen these relationships. If you come across an article or resource that might be useful to some-one, share it with them. Participating in networking events and online forums keeps you engaged and visible in your industry. These activities help you stay connected and, who knows, might even lead to new opportunities.

Tapping into your network for career opportunities takes a hands-on approach. Asking for informational interviews or job shad-owing opportunities can provide deeper insights into your areas of interest. These experiences allow you to learn more about the day-to-day responsibilities of a job and make a positive impres-sion on professionals in your industry. Requesting referrals or recommendations for job openings is another way to make use of your network. If you hear about a job opportunity that interests you, don't hesitate to ask a contact if they can refer you or provide a recommendation. Seeking someone to help mentor you, and so guide you, from a list of experienced professionals can also be incredibly valuable. Mentors can offer advice, share their experi-ences, and help you navigate the challenges of your career.

. . .

I've included a networking activity here, so you can see just how easy and creative it can be. Start by creating a list of five professionals in your desired field. Reach out to them with a personalized message expressing your interest in their work and asking if they would be open to a brief interview – like a fact-finding mission. Prepare a few questions in advance, such as "What do you enjoy most about your job?" or "What advice do you have for someone starting in this field?" This exercise will help you practice reaching out and build confidence in your networking abilities. And maybe it could lead to a real opportunity someday.

Networking is something great to get a handle on and can really give you the edge.

By understanding its importance, employing practical strategies, maintaining and expanding your network, and making use of these connections for opportunities, you set yourself up for long-term success.

To sum up, navigating your career journey involves exploring various options, crafting a compelling resume, mastering job interviews, and building a strong professional network. By focusing on these key areas, you'll be better equipped to pursue opportunities that align with your goals and create a solid foundation for success in your chosen field.

In the next chapter, we'll explore the skills needed to keep our homes running smoothly. So, go grab your hammer and let's get into it.

CHAPTER NINE

HOME MAINTENANCE PROFICIENCY

O h dear! Water seems to pouring from below the sink. What do we do first? Who do we call? At first, and being a young child, I panicked, asking myself questions like this, envisioning a flood of biblical proportions forcing its way through my beautiful home. My dad calmly walked over though, grabbed a wrench, and in a few minutes, the leak was fixed. That moment stuck with me. It was a clear demonstration of how knowing basic home maintenance and having the tools handy can prevent minor issues from becoming major disasters. This chapter will start by walking you through some essential plumbing skills, ensuring you're prepared to handle common household problems with confidence. We start here as plumbing tends to be something that many of us can get to grips with and these problems tend to arise more than other issues. Following this, we'll discuss electrical issues, resolving problems with home appliances and just, simply, keeping everything organized. Let's get started!

9.1 THE BASICS

Understanding the plumbing system in your home is the first step to making effective repairs. The system consists of several key components: pipes and fittings, valves and faucets, as well as drains and traps. Pipes and fittings are the backbone, transporting water throughout your home. They come in various materials like copper, PVC, and PEX, each with their own benefits and drawbacks. Valves and faucets control the flow of water, allowing you to turn it on and off as needed. Drains and traps, on the other hand, are responsible for carrying wastewater away from your sinks, showers, and toilets. They include U-shaped bends, known as traps, which prevent sewer gases from entering your home.

One common plumbing issue is a leaky faucet, which can waste a significant amount of water if not addressed promptly. Fixing a leaky faucet is a straightforward process that can save both water and money. Start by turning off the water supply to the faucet. This is usually done by closing the shut-off valves located under the sink. If there are no shut-off valves, you may need to turn off the main water supply to the house; every building will have one of these. Next, remove the faucet handle. This often involves unscrewing a small screw hidden under a decorative cap. Once the handle is off, you'll see all the inner workings. Most leaks are caused by worn-out washers or O-rings. Replace these with new ones, making sure they are the correct size and type for your faucet – you can ask at your local hardware store. Reassemble the faucet, turn the water supply back on, and test the faucet to ensure the leak is fixed.

. . .

Clogged drains are another common household issue that can get pretty annoying if left unchecked. Unclogging drains safely and effectively involves a few simple tools and techniques. For sinks and toilets, a plunger is often the tool of choice. Ensure there is enough water in the sink or toilet to cover the plunger's rubber cup. Place the plunger over the drain, creating a seal, and push down and pull up vigorously to dislodge the clog. If the plunger doesn't work, a drain snake can be employed for more stubborn clogs. It consists of a long, flexible metal cable with a coil or cutting head at the end that you insert into the drain to release whatever there may be blocking it up. Insert the snake into the drain and turn the handle to break up or retrieve the blockage. Avoid using chemical drain cleaners as they can damage pipes and are harmful to the environment.

Handling minor pipe leaks can temporarily prevent further damage until professional help is available. The first step is identifying the source of the leak. Look for water stains, dripping water, or damp areas along the pipe. Once you've located the leak, you can use pipe repair tape or epoxy putty for a temporary fix. Pipe repair tape, also known as self-fusing silicone tape, can be wrapped around the leaky area to create a watertight seal. Epoxy putty, on the other hand, is molded and pressed onto the leak, hardening to form a durable patch. Place a bucket under the leak to catch any drips and contact a plumber for a permanent solution.

The important thing is to stop problems from escalating into costly mishaps; so why not reach for your spanner, rather than your phone, when things go wrong? But let's make sure you've got all the gear to get started:

Plumbing Tool Checklist

- Pliers
- Pipe wrenches
- Teflon tape
- Plumber's snake
- Adjustable wrench
- Pipe repair tape
- Epoxy putty

Having these tools on hand will equip you to tackle most minor plumbing issues with ease and efficiency, saving time and meaning you can relax, knowing you've got these things to hand.

9.2 ELECTRICAL SAFETY AND SIMPLE FIXES

Understanding basic electrical safety is of paramount importance. Electricity powers our homes, but it can also pose serious risks if not managed correctly. The first rule of thumb is to always turn off the power before starting any electrical repair. This can be done at the breaker panel, which is usually located in the basement or a utility room. To ensure safety, use insulated tools specifically designed for electrical work. Avoid using metal tools, which can conduct electricity and cause shocks. It's also important to never overload outlets with too many devices. Overloading can lead to overheating and potentially cause a fire. Keep water and electrical appliances far apart, especially in kitchens and bathrooms, as water is a conductor and can lead to electric shocks or even electrocution.

Replacing a light bulb might seem simple, but doing it safely requires attention to detail. First, turn off the light switch to cut the power, or better yet, cut the breaker, as mentioned above. This is a basic yet crucial step to avoid electrical shocks. Next, choose the correct wattage and type of bulb. Using the wrong wattage can cause overheating and damage the fixture. Always check the fixture's label for recommended wattage. Use a sturdy ladder or step stool to reach the light fixture safely. Avoid using wobbly chairs or unstable surfaces that could lead to falls. Once you've removed the old bulb, dispose of it properly. Incandescent bulbs can go in the regular trash, but CFLs and LEDs often need to be recycled due to the materials they contain.

Resetting a circuit breaker is one of those things that sound complex, but is fairly simple to your head around. Again, find the breaker panel. On the panel, you'll see several switches. A tripped breaker will typically be in the "off" position or somewhere in the middle. To reset it, switch it fully to the "off" position, then back to "on." This should restore power to the specific area of your home; many breaker panels will have the part of the home they actually serve written on each of the breakers. It's always important to investigate why the breaker tripped in the first place though. Common causes include overloaded circuits or short circuits. If the breaker trips again immediately, you may need to unplug some devices to reduce the load or consult an electrician to check for more serious issues.

. . .

Fixing a faulty outlet requires a few steps but can be done safely with the right precautions. First and foremost, turn off the power to the outlet at the breaker panel. Double-check that the outlet is not live by using a voltage tester. Once you're sure it's safe, remove the outlet cover and screws. Check for loose or damaged wires inside. Loose wires can cause intermittent power or even sparks, while damaged wires might need replacing. Tighten any loose connections and replace any damaged components. Reassemble the outlet, making sure all screws and parts are securely in place. Turn the power back on at the breaker panel and test the outlet to ensure it's functioning correctly. Let's put the advice down here into a list; make sure to refer to it when necessary.

Electrical Safety Checklist

- Always turn off the power before starting any electrical repair.
- Use insulated tools specifically designed for electrical work.
- Never overload outlets with too many devices.
- Keep water and electrical appliances far apart.
- Use a voltage tester to ensure outlets are not live before working on them.
- Dispose of old bulbs properly, especially CFLs and LEDs that need recycling.

Being mindful of electrical safety rules and knowing how to perform simple fixes can prevent accidents and ensure your home remains safe and functional. It's important to say though that this is an area that if you don't feel comfortable doing something don't risk it and call a professional. The small savings you make won't be worth it if you're not around to enjoy the results.

9.3 MAINTAINING HOUSEHOLD APPLIANCES

We all need regular check-ups and the same goes for our beloved home appliances. Regular maintenance extends their lifespan and ensures they operate efficiently, saving you money on energy bills and repairs. One key aspect of maintenance is cleaning filters and vents. For instance, the lint filter in your dryer should be cleaned after every load to prevent fire hazards and improve drying efficiency. Similarly, air conditioner filters need regular cleaning to maintain airflow and cooling performance. Checking for wear and tear on appliances is a good tip. Look for frayed cords, loose parts, or any signs of damage that might need attention. Scheduling routine inspections, either by yourself or a professional, helps catch minor issues before they get worse.

A clean refrigerator not only looks good but also operates more efficiently. Start by removing all the food, then throw out the expired food and wipe down the shelves with a relatively mild multipurpose spray solution. Pay special attention to the corners and crevices where spills can accumulate. Cleaning the condenser coils, usually located at the back or bottom of the fridge, is essential. Dust and debris on the coils force the fridge to work harder, using more energy. Use a coil brush or vacuum to clean them thoroughly. Checking and adjusting the temperature settings can also improve efficiency. The ideal fridge temperature is between 37°F and 40°F, while the freezer should be at 0°F. If your refrigerator has a water dispenser or ice maker, remember to replace the water filter every six months to ensure clean water and ice.

The washing machine, an indispensable household appliance, also requires regular upkeep to make sure you get rid of all those nasty stains. Start by cleaning the detergent dispenser and drum. Detergent buildup can lead to mold and unpleasant odors, so it's important to clean these areas regularly. Simply remove the dispenser and wash it with warm, soapy water. For the drum, run an empty cycle with hot water and a cup of white vinegar or a washing machine cleaner to eliminate residue and bacteria. Checking the hoses for leaks or cracks is an important step. Over time, hoses can wear out or become brittle, leading to potential leaks. Replace any damaged hoses to prevent water damage. Aim to run a cleaning cycle once a month; trust me, it can save you a fortune further down the line.

Dishwashers are no different. Start by cleaning the filter and spray arms – those things that spin and spray the water. The filter traps food particles and debris, which can clog the system if not cleaned regularly. Remove the filter and rinse it under hot water. The spray arms may also contain trapped food. Use a small brush or toothpick to clear any blockages. Running a cleaning cycle with a dishwasher cleaner helps remove grease and limescale buildup. Additionally, check and refill the rinse aid dispenser to ensure your dishes come out sparkling clean. Inspecting and tightening any loose screws or fittings can prevent leaks and ensure the dishwasher operates efficiently.

. . .

Regular appliance maintenance might seem time-consuming, but it significantly prolongs the life of your devices and keeps them running efficiently. Cleaning filters, checking for wear and tear, and scheduling routine inspections can prevent many common issues. A well-maintained refrigerator, washing machine, and dishwasher not only perform better but also save you money on utility bills and repairs.

9.4 CLEANING AND ORGANIZING YOUR SPACE

Creating a cleaning schedule may seem like just another chore on top of the ones you already have, but it's a vital step in maintaining a tidy and hygienic living space. Start by breaking down your cleaning tasks into daily, weekly, and monthly routines. Daily tasks are the small but essential ones that keep your home from descending into chaos. Making your bed each morning sets a positive tone for the day and instantly makes your room look neater. Washing dishes after meals prevents the buildup of dirty dishes and keeps your kitchen sanitary. Ensure countertops are wiped down to avoid nasty pests wanting to rummage around your home.

Weekly tasks tackle the more intensive cleaning jobs that don't need daily attention but are crucial for maintaining a clean home. Vacuuming all carpeted areas and mopping hard floors remove dirt and allergens that accumulate throughout the week. Doing laundry regularly keeps your clothes fresh and stops you ending up with a giant mound at the end of a long period. Don't forget to clean the bathrooms—scrubbing toilets, sinks, and showers to eliminate soap scum and bacteria. Changing bed linens weekly ensures a clean and comfortable sleeping environment.

Monthly tasks focus on the deep cleaning that keeps your living space truly pristine. Cleaning windows lets in more natural light and improves your home's appearance. Dusting hard-to-reach areas like ceiling fans, light fixtures, and the tops of cabinets prevents the buildup of dust and allergens. Vacuuming under furniture and behind appliances can help remove hidden dirt and debris. This is also a good time to declutter areas that tend to collect random items, like junk drawers or closet corners. Try not to think these tasks as tedious from the outset, but put a positive spin on it, like "Now I finally have time to listen to that podcast or that radio show".

So, is it all about elbow grease or are there some specific and effective techniques we need to know? I would very much say it's the latter. Let's look at a few. Dusting and wiping down surfaces regularly prevents dust buildup and keeps your home looking fresh. Use a microfiber cloth or duster for furniture, shelves, and electronics. For floors, vacuuming is great for carpets, while mopping is essential for hard surfaces like tile or hardwood. Use a suitable cleaner for each type of flooring to avoid damage. Cleaning bathrooms involves scrubbing toilets, sinks, and showers with disinfectant cleaners to kill germs and remove soap scum. Remember, the more you do it, the less it will be like a scrub and more like a light wipe. For stubborn stains and grime, let the cleaner sit for a few minutes before scrubbing or wiping. This method is effective for removing tough spots without excessive force.

. . .

Decluttering and organizing your space can transform a chaotic environment into a functional and aesthetically pleasing one. Start by sorting items into keep, donate, and discard piles. This method helps you decide what's truly necessary and what's just taking up space. Use storage solutions like bins, shelves, and hooks to keep items organized and easily accessible. Label containers for quick identification, making it easier to find what you need without rummaging through everything. Regularly review and declutter your spaces to prevent the buildup of unnecessary items. This habit ensures that your home remains organized and clutter-free.

Maintaining a clean space requires ongoing effort but pays off. Give items a proper place and make sure they always find their place again after use. Cleaning up spills and messes immediately prevents stains and makes the cleaning process easier. Encourage roommates or family members to contribute to household chores. Creating a chore chart can help distribute tasks evenly and ensure everyone pitches in. Setting aside time for thorough cleaning keeps your home looking its best and prevents small messes from becoming overwhelming. Consistency is key!

A tidy home goes beyond just looking good—it helps create a cozy and healthy space to live in. Developing simple habits, like setting up a cleaning routine and picking up a few effective tips, can really help. Just keep in mind that staying organized is a continuous process, and a little effort here and there goes a long way.

CHAPTER TEN

DIGITAL LITERACY AND SAFETY

We are very much living in the computer age. The mouse is often described as an 'appendage' – like it's another part of our bodies, like a thumb or finger. And for screen time, find me a person who wouldn't like to reduce it. I got super excited setting up my first social media account. It felt like a one-way ticket to new people and shared experiences – and, it was to be fair. But, only a few days in to using my account, I posted something – let's say – inappropriate, and well a friend wasn't at all too pleased with me. It actually got me into trouble with the powers that be! Look, the internet is ace, but still we have to think a little about our digital footprint, i.e. what we do online, what we share and who we share it with. Let's cover some of these things now.

10.1 UNDERSTANDING OUR DIGITAL FOOTPRINT

A digital footprint is the trail of data you leave behind whenever you use the internet. It's like your online shadow, following you wherever you go. Every action you take online contributes to this footprint—whether you're posting a picture on Instagram, commenting on a friend's status, or even just browsing the web. For example, if you buy a pair of sneakers online, that purchase becomes part of your digital footprint, as does the search history which led up to the purchase. Even the apps you use and the websites you visit add to this ever-growing digital trail.

There are two main types of digital footprints: active and passive. Active footprints are the data traces you leave behind intentionally. These include the photos you upload, the tweets you send, and the blog posts you publish. Every time you actively share content or interact online, you're contributing to your active digital footprint. On the other hand, passive footprints are created without your direct input. This happens when websites collect information about you, such as your IP address, the type of device you're using, or your browsing history. This can also include cookies, stored by websites to track your activity and preferences.

The impacts of a digital footprint can be both positive and negative, influencing various aspects of your life. On the positive side, a well-managed digital footprint can enhance your personal and professional reputation. Colleges and employers often review applicants' online presence as part of their selection process. A history of responsible posts, meaningful engagements, and professional achievements can set you apart. On the flipside though, there are digital footprints—inappropriate comments, controversial posts, or questionable activities— which can lead to lost opportunities. There are numerous stories in fact where students have been denied enrolment to universities because of things they've posted, or things they've been involved in online.

What more, extensive digital footprints increase the risk of identity theft and privacy breaches, making it crucial to manage and protect your online presence.

It basically boils down to maintaining privacy and safeguarding your reputation. One effective strategy is to regularly review and update your privacy settings on social media platforms and other online accounts. These settings control who can see your posts, personal information, and activity. Adjusting them to restrict access to trusted friends and family can significantly reduce the likelihood of the wrong person seeing your online content. Another useful practice is to use incognito mode for sensitive browsing. This feature prevents your browser from saving your search history, cookies, and site data, offering a layer of privacy for activities you would simply prefer to keep confidential.

Deleting old accounts and unused apps is another way. Accounts you no longer use can still hold personal information, making them potential targets for hackers. By closing these accounts and removing obsolete apps, you reduce the data available about you online. Also, conducting periodic searches of your name online can help you monitor what information is publicly accessible. This simple yet powerful step allows you to see yourself from an outsider's perspective and take any necessary action before someone thinks to do the same thing.

Let's see now how well you're doing at controlling your online presence. Take a look and see if you are doing or have done any of the below things.

. . .

Digital Footprint Audit

1. **Review Privacy Settings:** Go through the privacy settings of all your social media accounts and adjust them to ensure only trusted contacts can view your information.
2. **Use Incognito Mode:** Practice using incognito mode for any sensitive online activities.
3. **Delete Old Accounts:** List all online accounts you no longer use and systematically delete them.
4. **Google Yourself:** Search your name online and note what information appears. Take steps to address any concerns you find.

By understanding and managing your digital footprint, you can navigate the online world more safely and responsibly. Your digital actions have long-lasting effects, so it's important to be mindful of what you share and how you interact online.

10.2 PROTECTING PERSONAL INFORMATION ONLINE

Understanding what constitutes personal information is something to we need to get to grips with first off. Personal information includes any data that can identify you. This ranges from obvious details like your full name, address, and phone number to more sensitive items like your Social Security number and banking details. Even seemingly harmless information, such as your birth date or school name, can be pieced together by malicious people to steal your identity or gain unauthorized access to your online accounts. Protecting this information is vital because once it's out there, it can be challenging to control how it's used or who has access to it.

Using strong and unique passwords for each of your accounts is one of the best ways to safeguard your personal information. Avoid simple passwords like "password123" or "qwerty" that are easy to guess. Instead, create complex passwords that combine letters, numbers, and special characters. For example, "T3ch!Savvy2023" is much harder to crack than a simple word. Consider using a password manager to keep track of your passwords and will in fact generate passwords for you automatically. Enabling two-factor authentication (2FA) adds an extra layer of security. This means you'll need to provide a second form of identification, such as a code sent to your phone, in addition to your password. This makes it much harder for someone to gain unauthorized access even if they have your password. Although it can take a few more minutes, it's worth it to know that you are surfing safely.

Avoid sharing personal information on public forums and social media platforms. It might seem fun to participate in quizzes or share updates about your life, but these can reveal details that scammers love to get their hands on. For example, those seemingly harmless quizzes asking about your first pet or favorite teacher can provide answers to common security questions. Always be cautious with emails and links from unknown sources. 'Phishing' attempts often disguise themselves as trustworthy messages from banks or social media sites, urging you to click a link or provide personal information. These emails usually have urgent language, suspicious links, or requests for personal information. If something feels off, don't click on any links. Instead, go directly to the website from your browser or report the email to the service provider. You might think it's hard to fall for such scams, but you'd be surprised just how authentic some of the messages look.

Using secure connections is another great way to stay safe online. Always ensure that the websites you visit are secure by looking for "https" in the URL and a padlock icon in the address bar. The "s" in "https" stands for secure, indicating that the website encrypts your data, making it harder for hackers to intercept. Avoid using public Wi-Fi for sensitive transactions like banking or shopping. Public networks are often less secure, making it easier for hackers to access your data. If you must use public Wi-Fi, consider using a virtual private network (VPN). A VPN encrypts your internet connection, adding an extra layer of security and making it more difficult for anyone to intercept your data.

By understanding what constitutes personal information and implementing these best practices, you can significantly reduce the risk of your data being stolen and used without your permission. Safeguarding your personal information online is as much about the immediate threats as it is about those which can strike further down the line. Whether it's creating strong passwords, recognizing phishing attempts, or using secure connections, every step you take can add an extra layer of protection.

10.3 RECOGNIZING AND AVOIDING ONLINE SCAMS

Like phishing, scams can be tricky to spot, especially when they come disguised as legitimate opportunities. One common type of scam is the online shopping scam. Imagine finding a website selling the latest sneakers at a fraction of the usual price. It seems too good to pass up, but after making the purchase, the shoes never arrive. This scenario is all too common. Scammers create fake websites that look professional to lure you in. They might even send counterfeit products or nothing at all. Always check the website's reviews and verify its authenticity before making any purchases.

Scams that promote job offers are another widespread concern. These scams often promise high-paying jobs that require little to no experience. They might ask for personal information or upfront fees for training materials. For example, you might receive an email offering you a job as a "secret shopper" or a remote data entry clerk. If an email looks legitimate, but it asks for your Social Security number or a fee to get started, approach with caution. Genuine employers will never ask for personal information or money upfront. Always research the company and verify job offers through official channels before providing any details.

Scams relating to romantic offers too are common. Scammers create fake profiles on dating sites and social media platforms, pretending to be someone they're not (you may have heard of the term "catfish" to describe this). They build a relationship with you over time, gaining your trust. Eventually, they ask for money, often citing emergencies like medical bills or travel expenses to come and visit you. It's easy to get caught up in the emotions, but always be cautious if someone you've never met in person asks for money. Verify their identity through video calls and be skeptical of any financial requests.

Lottery and prize scams are another trap. You'll receive a message claiming you've won a contest or lottery you never entered. All you need to do is pay a small fee to claim your prize. This scam preys on the excitement of winning something valuable. Legitimate lotteries and contests don't ask for money to claim a prize. If you receive such a message, it's almost certainly a scam and you know what you to do – ignore/delete.

Certain warning signs can help you identify these scams. As mentioned in all cases, requests for personal or financial information are major red flags. Legitimate organizations won't ask for sensitive details via email or messaging apps. High-pressure tactics to make immediate decisions are another sign. Scammers often create a sense of urgency to prevent you from thinking things through. Poor grammar and spelling in communications can also be a giveaway. While not all scams have these issues, many do. Finally, unverifiable contact information should raise suspicion. If you can't find a legitimate phone number or address for the organization, it's best to steer clear.

If you encounter a scam or suspect you've been targeted, take immediate action. Stop all communication with the scammer to avoid further manipulation. Report the scam to relevant authorities like the Federal Trade Commission (FTC) or your local law enforcement. Inform the affected service provider or platform so they can take appropriate measures. Monitor your financial accounts for any suspicious activity to catch any unauthorized transactions early. These steps can help mitigate the damage and prevent others from falling victim to the same trap.

If you do have to use your cards online, verify the legitimacy of websites and businesses before making the transaction. Look for reviews, check for secure connections, and ensure the business has a physical address and customer service number. Be skeptical of unsolicited offers and requests, especially those that seem too good to be true. Keep your personal information private and secure, sharing it only with trusted individuals and entities. Educating yourself and staying informed about new hacks can give you an advantage. Scammers constantly adapt their tactics, so staying updated can help you recognize and avoid new threats.

10.4 MANAGING SOCIAL MEDIA RESPONSIBLY

Social media has become an integral part of our lives, but it comes with its own set of challenges and responsibilities. The impact of social media on your life can be profound, affecting everything from your privacy to your mental health and even your future opportunities. Cyberbullying and online harassment are things to be aware of as we enter this online world. They can severely impact mental health, leading to anxiety, depression, and even suicidal thoughts. If you have problems in this regard, it's important to limit your interactions and speak to someone about the problems you've been facing. The truth is that not everyone at there is just looking for fun, and to be sociable – we must stay vigilant. Remember, as previously discussed, there exist nowadays a range of privacy settings on all forms of social media to help curtail the chances of coming into contact with those who just want to abuse.

It takes a proactive approach often to resolve these issues. Recognize the signs of cyberbullying, which can include receiving threatening messages, being excluded from online groups, or having rumors spread about you. If you encounter abusive users, block and report them immediately. Most social media platforms have built-in tools for reporting harassment. Seeking support from trusted adults or professionals is vital. Talk to a parent, teacher, or counselor about what you're experiencing. Document incidents and preserve evidence by taking screenshots or saving messages. This can be useful if you need to report the behavior to authorities or platform administrators. Cyberbullying is a serious issue, but you don't have to face it alone. There are resources and people ready to help you navigate these challenges.

Presenting a positive and authentic online persona is what we should all aspire to. It's not just about avoiding negative posts but also about actively showcasing your achievements, passions, and values. This helps build a reputation that reflects well on you in both personal and professional spheres. I'd recommend ensuring only trusted friends and family can see your personal information and updates.

Best practices for posting online can help you maintain a positive digital footprint. Always think before you post. Consider the long-term impact of your words and images. Avoid sharing sensitive or personal information that could be used against you. Be respectful and kind in your communications. Negative comments or heated arguments can escalate quickly and leave a lasting negative impression. Try to fact-check information before sharing it to avoid spreading misinformation; social media is a powerful tool, but it should be used responsibly. Your posts should reflect your best self, highlighting your achievements and values.

Understanding the impact of social media, effectively dealing with cyberbullying, setting privacy controls, and following best practices for posting are all crucial steps in managing your online presence responsibly. Social media offers incredible opportunities for connection and self-expression, but it also requires careful management to ensure that it benefits rather than harms you.

Next, we will explore how to build independence, covering topics such as living on a budget, navigating public transportation, and renting your first apartment. These skills are essential for becoming an adult and taking control of your life.

CHAPTER ELEVEN

BUILDING INDEPENDENCE

W hen I was seventeen, I got my first real taste of responsibility when my parents asked me to plan a family trip. They gave me a budget and told me to handle everything—gas, food, activities, you name it. At first, it felt like a lot to juggle, but as I started breaking it down, I realized I was actually having fun with it. That experience really opened my eyes to how important budgeting and planning are, and it was one of the first times I felt like I was stepping into something bigger – a place where I was treated like a responsible and independent individual.

11.1 LIVING ON A BUDGET

In many ways, being financially independent is the same as being independent; as we move towards adulthood, the money that we have available to buy things and pay for services, i.e. disposable income, is what feeds into being happy and contented and, well, free! As we've mentioned previously, it's vital to budget, to categorize exactly what we're spending using apps or other tools.

Budgeting with the aim of being independent is no different; it concerns thinking about one of those categories in terms of exactly how you can be the best, most independent you. On the other hand, living on that budget takes other skills. Let's cover some of these topics in more detail.

Budgeting for things that foster independence, like courses or driving lessons, is an investment in your future. These skills open doors to greater freedom and opportunities. For instance, learning to drive provides the independence to travel on your own terms, while enrolling in a course can enhance your career prospects or personal development. By setting aside money for these growth-oriented expenses, you're prioritizing long-term benefits that improve your quality of life. Budgeting for self-improvement not only helps you gain new skills but also builds confidence, empowering you to take charge of your own journey toward independence.

Let's look at one technique that may give us the upper edge when it comes to setting aside cash. The envelope system is effective method for this. Allocate money into different envelopes for each category, and once the money is gone, you know you've hit your limit for that category. Setting aside money for savings and emergencies can even form part of this. You'll probably want to aim for about 10% of your income. Just ensure you don't touch this envelope until when it's truly needed.

Whilst you want to be spending on things that allow you to live your best life - going out, parties, dates -tracking and adjusting your budget regularly ensures you stay on course with your other commitments. Keep receipts and record your expenses daily or weekly to avoid any surprises at the end of the month. If you're looking to spend money on things that will fuel your independence, especially things like a car, or workshops, then always shop around and try to get the best deals on things. It might require you to do some investigative work, but in the end it's really worth it if you can get big discounts.

Saving money while living on a budget can be challenging but it's definitely doable with some practical tips and strategies. Cooking at home instead of eating out can save you a significant amount of money. For example, a homemade meal might cost $5, while dining out could easily cost $20 or even $30. Going shopping during the sales and using coupons can reduce your grocery bills. Websites and apps like Honey and Rakuten can help you find deals and cashback offers. Sharing expenses with roommates or family members can also lighten the financial load. Splitting the cost of rent, utilities, and groceries makes living more affordable. Avoiding impulse purchases is another key strategy. Before making a purchase, ask yourself if it's something you need or just something you want. Waiting 24 hours before buying can help you avoid unnecessary spending. This is especially important now that buying things online takes just a few simple clicks.

Living on a Budget Exercise

Take a few moments now to have a good think about how you manage your current budget.

. . .

1. **List Your Priorities**: Identify three things that will help you become more independent (e.g., driving lessons, a course, or a new laptop).

2. **Evaluate Your Spending**: Review your last month's expenses. Are you spending on things that align with your independence goals? Write down any unnecessary expenses you could cut back on.

3. **Set a Savings Goal**: Choose one priority from your list and determine how much money you need to set aside each month to reach it.

Action: Start tracking your spending today and make adjustments to work toward your independence goals.

Achieving financial independence through careful budgeting requires discipline. By categorizing expenses, setting savings goals, and prioritizing investments in personal growth—like courses or driving lessons—you can build a foundation for long-term freedom. Tools like the envelope system help maintain control over spending, while strategies like cooking at home and avoiding impulse purchases can save money. Regularly reviewing and adjusting your budget ensures that you stay aligned with your independence goals. With the right approach, living on a budget becomes a powerful tool for creating the life you want and becoming the most independent version of yourself.

11.2 NAVIGATING PUBLIC TRANSPORTATION

You may already have a wealth of experience here, but it all depends on how you grew up. For me personally, I hadn't even been on a bus until I went to college – in fact, the first bus I tried to catch zoomed straight past me; no one told me that I had to flag it down! Because of this, let's quickly cover the basics. Buses and trains are two of the most common forms of public transportation. Buses are great for getting around town, while trains often cover longer distances or connect different parts of a city. Subways and light rail systems operate similarly to trains but are usually confined to urban areas, offering a quick way to navigate city centers. Ride-sharing services like Uber and Lyft provide flexibility and convenience, especially when public transport isn't available, but of course, they may cost a pretty penny. Biking and walking are also excellent alternatives, promoting both physical health and environmental sustainability.

Reading and understanding schedules is crucial for effective planning. Bus and train timetables display the times vehicles will arrive at specific stops. For example, a timetable might show that Bus 22 arrives at Main Street at 8:15 AM, 8:45 AM, and so on. Route maps help you understand the path a bus or train will take, including all the stops along the way. Using transit apps and websites can provide real-time information about delays or changes, ensuring you stay updated. These tools can also help you plan trips with multiple transfers, showing you exactly where and when to switch buses or trains to reach your destination efficiently.

Purchasing tickets and passes involves a few different options. Single-ride tickets are suitable for occasional travelers, while monthly passes offer savings for regular commuters. Many cities offer transit cards, which you can load with money and use for multiple rides, eliminating the need to buy a ticket each time. Mobile payment apps offer another convenient option, allowing you to purchase and store tickets on your smartphone. When buying tickets, be aware of fare zones, as traveling through multiple zones may increase the cost. Many transit systems offer discounts for students, so carrying your student ID can save you money.

Safety is paramount when using public transportation. Always stay aware of your surroundings, especially in crowded or unfamiliar areas. Keep personal belongings secure by holding them close or placing them between your feet. Avoid empty carriages or buses late at night, opting instead to sit near the driver or other passengers. Familiarize yourself with emergency procedures and exits, so you know what to do in case something goes wrong.

Public Transportation Safety Tips:

- Plan your trip in advance, knowing exact times, locations, and the amount of money needed for fares.
- Inform a family member or friend of your travel route

and schedule, and contact them when you leave and arrive at your destination.

- Have the exact fare amount to avoid displaying extra cash.
- Use well-lit and busy areas to wait for transport
- Sit in an aisle seat to observe surroundings and avoid being "boxed in."
- Sit near the driver or operator, but avoid seats next to the door to prevent theft.
- Stay alert and avoid dozing off or getting too distracted.
- Keep your belongings in your lap, on your arm, or between your feet, not on an empty seat.
- Avoid displaying expensive-looking watches, rings, necklaces, or other jewelry.
- Be aware of noisy passengers causing commotion, as it could be a staged diversion for theft.
- Observe the behavior of others around you; if you feel uneasy or threatened, change your seat and/or alert the driver.

11.3 RENTING YOUR FIRST APARTMENT

Searching for an apartment for the first time felt like a never-ending and fruitless endeavor for me. I think I soon got the hang of it though and don't doubt you will too. I include it here as it is something which can really put a strain on your finances. Some renters in major cities spend over 60% of their salary on rent! Start by setting a budget for rent and utilities. Consider your monthly income and determine what you can afford without stretching your finances too thin. A general rule is to spend no more than 30% of your income on rent. Once you have a budget, choose a location that's convenient for your daily commute. Proximity to work or school can save you time and transportation costs. Online rental platforms like Zillow and Craigslist are great resources to find listings that fit your criteria. Don't just rely on online photos; schedule a viewing to see the apartments in person – consider taking pictures or recording videos that you can play back later to remind yourself and maybe get some input from loved ones. During the tours, ask questions about utility costs, maintenance policies, and any other concerns you might have. Remember that renting by yourself can be very costly – you end up not just paying more rent, but paying the lion's share for every-thing, from bills to repairs when they crop up. If you decide to live with others, you can share costs, but it might be a good idea to think about just how many others you'd feel comfortable sharing with.

Understanding lease agreements is crucial before you sign on the dotted line. A lease is a legally binding contract, so you need to know what you're agreeing to. Pay attention to the lease terms and duration, which specify how long you'll be renting the apart-ment. Most leases are for 12 months, but some might be for a shorter or longer period. Security deposits are usually required and serve as a financial cushion for the landlord in case of damages or unpaid rent. Make sure you understand the rent payment schedule and any late fees associated with it. Addition-ally, the lease should outline maintenance responsibilities. Know who to contact for repairs and what is expected from you in terms of keeping the property in good condition. Be aware of the rules for breaking the lease or early termination. Some leases have strict penalties, while others might be more flexible.

· · ·

Preparing for the move-in is an exciting yet busy time. Start by creating a moving checklist to stay organized. This list should include tasks like packing, labeling boxes, and arranging for movers or renting a moving truck. Packing systematically can make the process smoother. Label boxes by room and contents to make unpacking easier. Arrange for utilities such as electricity, gas, and water to be set up before you move in. Don't forget to arrange for an internet service provider (ISP) to get you connected, as this is essential for both work and leisure. Cleaning your new apartment before moving in can also make the transition more comfortable. Take photos of the apartment's condition to document any pre-existing damage, which can help ensure you get your security deposit back.

Handling maintenance requests promptly can prevent minor issues from becoming major ones. Report any maintenance needs to your landlord as soon as possible. Building good relationships with roommates and neighbors can make your living experience more enjoyable. Clear communication about shared responsibilities and expenses helps avoid conflicts. Budgeting for household expenses is also essential. Create a system for splitting costs like rent, utilities, and groceries to ensure everyone contributes fairly and bills are paid on time.

11.4 BASIC AUTOMOTIVE MAINTENANCE

In terms of not incurring unnecessary costs, knowing a little about your car can mean big savings. The engine and transmission are the heart and soul of your car, let's start here and work our way through some key areas. Regular oil changes keep the engine lubricated and running efficiently. Next, the braking system is crucial for your safety. It consists of brake pads, rotors, and fluid, which all need regular checks. The electrical system powers everything from your headlights to your battery. Keeping an eye on these components ensures you won't be left stranded. Tires and suspension are equally important. Tires provide traction, while the suspension system ensures a smooth ride by absorbing shocks from the road.

Performing routine maintenance can keep your vehicle in top shape. Start with checking and changing the oil. This should be done every 3,000 to 5,000 miles, depending on your car and driving habits. Regular oil changes prevent engine wear and improve performance. Replacing air filters ensures your engine gets clean air, enhancing fuel efficiency, which again can save costs. Air filters should be checked every six months. Inspecting and rotating tires every 6,000 to 8,000 miles promotes even wear and extends tire life. Uneven tire wear can lead to alignment issues and decreased fuel efficiency. Checking fluid levels, such as coolant, brake fluid, and windshield washer fluid can, if low, cause overheating or brake failure or the possibility of a dangerous journey on your way home if you can't see what's in front of the window screen. Always add to the recommended levels. Whether you can do these tasks yourself depends on how willing you are to get your hands dirty. For me personally, I change the air filters, and I rotate the tires, but I get the local garage to change the tires and do things like oil changes. The things described below though should be achievable by just about anyone with patience and the right tools.

. . .

Knowing how to jump-start a dead battery is a valuable skill. You'll need jumper cables and another car with a working battery. Attach the positive cable to the positive terminal of the dead battery and the other end to the positive terminal of the good battery. Then, attach the negative cable to the negative terminal of the good battery and the other end to a clean, unpainted metal surface on the car with the dead battery. Start the working car and let it run for a few minutes before trying to start the dead car. Changing a flat tire is another essential skill. Make sure you have a spare tire, jack, and lug wrench in your car. Loosen the lug nuts, lift the car with the jack, remove the flat tire, and replace it with the spare. Tighten the lug nuts securely before lowering the car. Replacing windshield wipers is simple but crucial for visibility. Lift the wiper arm, press the release tab, and slide the old blade off. Attach the new blade by sliding it onto the arm until it clicks.

One thing that often gets overlooked is addressing warning lights on the dashboard. Managing this can promptly prevent minor issues from becoming major problems. Refer to your vehicle's manual to understand what each warning light means and take appropriate action. Again, depending on the issue, it might be good to get various quotes from mechanics for the work that needs doing, or check online to get a rough estimate of what others tend to pay for the work to make sure you're not overpaying.

More important that just about anything is to stay safe. We like to save money and budget but we should be driving a car that is in a drivable condition. Conducting pre-trip inspections can prevent unexpected issues and save you money having to call out the tow truck. Check your lights, tires, and mirrors before hitting the road. Make sure all lights are working, tires are properly inflated, and mirrors are adjusted for optimal visibility, especially for longer journeys. Keeping an emergency kit in your car is a good idea. Include items like jumper cables, a first aid kit, a flashlight, and basic tools. This prepares you for unexpected situations.

Traffic signals and laws are there for your safety and the safety of others – remember to follow them. Always obey speed limits, use turn signals, and never drive under the influence of alcohol or drugs. Knowing when to seek professional help for repairs is vital. If you're unsure about a problem or it's beyond your skill level, consult a mechanic. Regular professional inspections can also catch issues you might miss.

In summary, learning how to effectively budget, navigating public transportation, renting your first apartment and basic automotive maintenance are all vital skills for adult life. By understanding finances, reading up on transportation schedules, budgeting effectively for rent, and performing simple car maintenance, you can save time, money, and avoid unnecessary stress. Safety remains a top priority in many of these areas, whether it's staying alert on public transit, knowing your rights as a tenant, or keeping your car in good working condition. With preparation and attention to detail, you'll be well-equipped to manage these responsibilities confidently.

CHAPTER TWELVE

PERSONAL GROWTH AND SELF-REFLECTION

When I was in my final year of high school, I remember feeling lost and unsure about my future. I had dreams and aspirations, but they seemed vague and unattainable. One day, a mentor suggested that I start setting personal goals. Skeptical at first, I decided to give it a go. I began by writing down exactly what I wanted to achieve by the end of the school year. This simple but effective act of putting my goals down on paper gave me a sense of direction and purpose that I hadn't felt before. As weeks passed, I noticed a change in my attitude and performance. This experience highlighted the powerful impact of goal-setting on personal growth and motivation. By setting clear objectives, I was able to focus my efforts more effectively and turn ambitions into actionable steps. It reinforced the idea that structured goals serve as both a guide and a motivator, helping to drive progress even in challenging times. Let's see how this is done.

12. 1 SETTING PERSONAL GOALS

How do we grow and improve ourselves? Well, understanding exactly what we mean by goal-setting is a great place to start. Goals provide direction and focus, making it easier to navigate through life's uncertainties. When you set a goal, you give yourself a target to aim for, which helps in organizing your efforts and resources efficiently. This focus can enhance your self-discipline, as you're more likely to stay committed to your tasks when you see them as steps toward a larger objective. Moreover, measuring your progress and achievements along the way can be incredibly motivating, giving you tangible proof of your hard work paying off. This, in turn, builds your self-confidence, as you realize that you can set and achieve goals, no matter how challenging they may seem. It's about sticking with it.

There are different types of personal goals, but let's zero in on short-term and long-term goals and how they can help you plan more effectively. Short-term goals are those that you can achieve in the near future, such as within a day, week, or month. These might include tasks like starting a new habit, creating a study routine, or saving a small amount of money. You might set a short-term goal to read for 30 minutes every day for a month or something similar to this. Long-term goals, on the other hand, are more extensive and require a longer period to accomplish, typically ranging from a year to many decades. Examples include graduating from high school, learning a new language, or following a particular career path. Achieving academic success, building healthy habits, and personal development are all examples of long-term goals that require sustained effort and commitment.

. . .

Creating effective goals involves using the SMART framework that we've mentioned in previous chapters. It means thinking about goals in terms of how they are Specific, Measurable, Achievable, Relevant, and Time-bound. Tracking and adjusting your goals is an essential part of the goal-setting process. Regularly reviewing and reflecting on your progress allows you to see how far you've come and identify areas where you may need to make adjustments. Life is unpredictable, and sometimes unforeseen challenges can arise. Being flexible and willing to adjust your goals based on these changes is crucial for maintaining momentum. Celebrating your achievements, no matter how small, can boost your motivation and reinforce your commitment to your goals. Learning from setbacks is equally important; it provides valuable lessons that can help you improve and grow.

Why not take the time now to look at the SMART Goals framework below. Get yourself comfortable, and on a piece of paper, note down your answers. Remember not to make the goal too unrealistic and stay positive about your capacity to achieve it.

SMART Goals Framework

- **Specific:** What exactly do you want to achieve?
- **Measurable:** How will you know when you've achieved it?
- **Achievable:** Is it realistic and within your capabilities?
- **Relevant:** Does it align with your broader objectives?
- **Time-bound:** When do you want to achieve it by?

. . .

By setting, tracking, and adjusting your goals using these strategies, you can progress in terms of personal growth and self-improvement. The process not only helps you achieve your objectives but also develops essential skills like self-discipline, time management, and staying strong, which are vital in all areas of life.

12.2 JOURNALING FOR SELF-REFLECTION

Have you ever kept a diary? Did you write yourself letters as a kid? This is not all that different really and it's taking the world by storm as a powerful tool for enhancing self-awareness, reducing stress and anxiety, improving problem-solving skills, and encouraging personal growth and creativity. When you put pen to paper, you create a safe space to explore your thoughts and feelings without judgment. This practice allows you to get in touch with your innermost self, helping you recognize patterns in your behavior and emotions. Over time, you begin to understand what triggers certain reactions and how to navigate them better.

Doing this also serves as an outlet for stress and anxiety, giving you a chance to blow off steam and process the angst you might be having concerning a particular issue. As you write, you might find that solutions to problems become clearer, as the act of organizing your thoughts in this way can lead to new insights. Additionally, the creative freedom that comes with journaling can inspire innovative ideas and personal growth, pushing you to explore new aspects of yourself and your abilities.

. . .

There are various types of journals, each serving a unique purpose. A daily diary is perfect for recording everyday experiences, providing a chronological account of your life that you can look back on. This type of journal helps you track day-to-day changes and progress. Lastly, a goal-setting journal is designed to track your personal objectives, breaking them down into manageable steps and milestones. This type of journal keeps you focused and motivated, ensuring that you stay on track to achieve your goals.

Free writing, also known as stream-of-consciousness journaling, involves writing continuously without worrying about grammar, content or structure. This technique allows your thoughts to flow freely, often leading to surprising revelations. Prompt-based journaling uses a range of interesting questions to guide your writing. Prompts like "What are you most proud of today?" or "What challenges did you face this week?" can help you dive deeper into specific topics. Bullet journaling combines organization and creativity, using bullet points, symbols, and color coding to track tasks, goals, and habits. This method is especially useful for those who enjoy a structured yet flexible approach. Reflective journaling encourages you to analyze your emotions and experiences, providing a space to process events and their impact on you. This type of journaling can lead to deeper self-understanding and growth.

Incorporating journaling into your daily routine doesn't have to be complicated. The key is to dedicate just a little time each day, whether it's in the morning to set intentions for the day or at night to reflect on your experiences – or both! Creating a comfortable and inspiring journaling space can make the practice more enjoyable. Choose a quiet spot where you can relax and focus, and consider adding elements like candles, soft lighting, or soothing music. You can use either digital or traditional journals based on your preference. Some people love the tactile experience of writing by hand, while others prefer the convenience and organization of digital apps, a Word document. Combining journaling with other self-care practices, such as meditation or reading, can enhance the benefits. For instance, you might meditate for a few minutes to clear your mind before journaling, or read a few pages of an inspiring book to spark new ideas, or go back and recap your concerns from the previous day.

Why not set yourself this exercise for some point today? Or, if you're feeling in the mood, why not go for it now and let your mind wander?

Journaling Prompt Exercise

- Start your journal with the prompt: "What are three things I learned about myself today?" Write freely for at least ten minutes, allowing your thoughts to flow without self-criticism. This exercise can open up new avenues of self-reflection and help you uncover insights that might otherwise remain hidden.

12.3 DEVELOPING A GROWTH MINDSET

A growth mindset, as the name suggests, concerns a certain amount of advancing – of pushing forward, as opposed to a fixed mindset, which secures you in one place. It's the belief that your abilities and intelligence can be developed through effort, learning, and perseverance. It encourages you to see challenges as opportunities to grow, to learn and to strive. For example, someone with a growth mindset might say, "I can improve with practice." On the other hand, a fixed mindset is the belief that your abilities and intelligence are static and so cannot be changed. People with this mindset often avoid challenges for fear of failure and might say, "I'm just not good at this." Understanding these differences is crucial for personal development, as your mindset can significantly impact your motivation, fortitude, and overall success.

Adopting this mindset offers numerous benefits that can positively influence various aspects of your life. One of the most significant advantages is increased resilience and perseverance. When you believe that you can improve through effort, you're more likely to stick with challenging tasks and not give up easily. This mindset also enhances your learning and skill development, as you're more open to feedback and willing to put in the work to improve. What more, it can fosters a greater willingness to take on challenges. Instead of avoiding difficult tasks, you see them as opportunities to learn and grow. This perspective also leads to improved problem-solving and creativity, as you're more likely to explore different solutions and think outside the box when faced with obstacles.

· · ·

Cultivating such an attitude involves practical strategies that you can incorporate into your daily life. One of the first steps is to embrace challenges and view failures as learning opportunities. Instead of seeing a setback as a dead end, consider what you can learn from the experience and how you can apply that knowledge to similar events which may rise in the future. Focusing on the process rather than the outcome is another effective strategy. This means valuing the effort and learning that goes into a task, regardless of the final result. Seeking feedback and using it constructively is also crucial. Whether it's from teachers, peers, or mentors, feedback can provide valuable insights that help you improve. Practicing self-compassion and positive self-talk is equally important. Give yourself a boost with affirmations like, "I can get better with practice," and be kind to yourself when you make mistakes.

Using a growth mindset in everyday situations can really change how you handle new experiences and challenges. It helps you stay open to learning and makes tough moments feel more manageable. When starting a new hobby or subject at school or college, approach it with curiosity and openness. Instead of worrying about being perfect right away, focus on exploring and enjoying the learning process. Reflecting on past experiences to identify areas for growth is another useful practice. Think about times when you overcame challenges and what you learned from those experiences. Surrounding yourself with supportive buddies can also make a big difference. Find those who celebrate your successes with you! Leave behind those who look on with jealousy.

. . .

Adopting a growth mindset can change the way you see life. When you understand that skills and intelligence can improve with effort, new possibilities open up. This mindset helps you face challenges with strength and learn from them. Whether you're dealing with schoolwork, personal problems, or new opportunities, a growth mindset gives you the confidence to see each challenge as a chance to learn and do better. It doesn't always come over night, but it's about taking small steps to closer towards it.

12.4 PRACTICING GRATITUDE

A friend of mine gave me a wonderful tip. She told me that every time she steps in the shower, and the water touches her face, she reels off four to five different things she's grateful for that day. After time, she says that the body ends up associating the feeling of water with positivity. I think this is a wonderful way, and shows how we can make simple connections between mind and body.

Gratitude is what she is practicing in these moments. It's about recognizing and appreciating the good things in life, no matter how small. When you practice gratitude, you shift your focus from what you lack to what you have, which can significantly improve your mental and emotional well-being. Appreciating the positives in your life can enhance your relationships by making you more likely to express thankfulness towards others. This, in turn, strengthens social connections. It can also reduce stress and boost happiness, serving as a powerful antidote to negative emotions. By focusing on the good, you train your brain to look for positive patterns, which can improve overall mental health and resilience.

. . .

Incorporating gratitude into your daily life can be simple yet profoundly impactful. One effective method is keeping a gratitude journal, where you jot down things you're thankful for each day. This practice can shift your mindset over time, making you more aware of the positive things that surround you. Expressing gratitude to others, whether through letters or verbal appreciation, can also make a big difference. It not only makes the other person feel valued but also strengthens your relationship with them. Reflecting on positive experiences and moments before bed can help end your day on a high note, making it easier to sleep peacefully. You can also participate in gratitude challenges or activities, such as writing thank-you notes or sharing what you're grateful for with friends and family. These practices can make gratitude a more essential part of your life.

In this chapter, we've explored the transformative power of setting personal goals, journaling for self-reflection, cultivating a growth mindset, and practicing gratitude. Each of these tools can help you stay focused, motivated, and resilient as you navigate life's challenges. By setting clear objectives, reflecting on your progress, embracing challenges with a growth mindset, and appreciating the positives, you'll be better equipped to promote personal growth and achieve your aspirations. These practices offer a holistic approach to self-improvement, encouraging both emotional and mental well-being.

CONCLUSION

By having read through until now, you've embarked on a journey of self-discovery and growth, guided by the intent to build independence, confidence, and practical skills. You've set yourself the goal of exploring various aspects of life that are crucial for thriving as a teen or young adult. Each chapter has been a stepping stone, leading you towards becoming more prepared for the real world.

In Chapter 1, we began with financial literacy, an essential skill for managing your money wisely. You learned how to create a personal budget, understand bank accounts, and grasp the basics of credit and taxes. These skills lay the foundation for making informed financial decisions throughout your life.

Next, in Chapter 2, we delved into healthy cooking skills. From mastering kitchen tools and safety to cooking nutritious meals, understanding nutrition labels, and planning groceries, you've gained the confidence to take charge of your diet and health.

Time management was another critical area we explored in Chapter 3. You learned to set SMART goals, prioritize tasks, and create effective schedules. These techniques will help you balance your responsibilities, reduce stress, and increase productivity.

Personal hygiene and grooming were covered in detail in Chapter 4, emphasizing daily routines, skincare, hair care, and how we can dress differently depending on the occasion. These habits are vital for maintaining a healthy lifestyle and making positive impressions in social and professional settings.

The chapter on emergency preparedness – Chapter 5 - equipped you with essential first aid skills and strategies for handling household emergencies, natural disasters, and creating emergency plans. Being prepared for the unexpected is just a fundamental part of life.

In Chapter 6, we focused also on mental health support, recognizing and managing stress, practicing anxiety relief techniques, building emotional resilience, and knowing when to seek professional help. I wish you all who read this excellent mental health – just remember to prioritize these aspects of your experience and you'll do fine!

Chapter 7 concerned the development of social skills, another key area, where you learned effective communication, building and maintaining friendships, navigating romantic relationships, and resolving conflicts. Such social skills are needed for personal and professional success.

Career readiness, in Chapter 8, was a comprehensive section, guiding you through how to explore the many different career options available to you, writing compelling resumes, mastering job interviews, and building a professional network. These steps are crucial for launching and advancing your career.

The suggestions on how to best maintain your home in Chapter 9 taught you basic plumbing repairs, electrical safety, maintaining household appliances, and keeping your living space clean and organized. These practical skills ensure you can handle everyday household challenges.

In Chapter 10, we focused on digital literacy and safety surrounding the best way to manage your digital footprint, protecting your personal information, recognizing and avoiding online scams, and using social media responsibly. Navigating the digital world safely is essential in today's technology-driven society – safe surfing!

Chapter 11 explored essential skills for adult life focused on building independence. These included being aware of how we manage our budgets, navigating public transportation, renting your first apartment, and basic automotive maintenance. With the right preparation and attention, you'll confidently manage these responsibilities.

Finally, in Chapter 12, we discussed personal growth and self-reflection, emphasizing setting personal goals, journaling, developing a growth mindset, and practicing gratitude for yourself and those around you. These are skills that require commitment, but they are so valuable as we enter the various stages of our adult lives.

As you move forward, continue to apply these skills in your daily life. The journey doesn't end here. Life is a continuous learning process, and the skills you've gained will serve as a strong foundation. Keep setting goals, seeking new knowledge, and challenging yourself to grow further.

Remember, you have the ability to thrive and succeed. With the knowledge and skills you've acquired, you're well-equipped to face the challenges of the real world. Believe in yourself, stay committed to your own personal growth, and embrace the opportunities that come your way.

I believe in you, and I know you're capable of amazing things. This is just the start of your journey towards independence and growth, and the future is full of endless possibilities. Keep moving forward with determination and a positive outlook. You have the strength to shape your own path and build a life that truly fulfills you.

Thanks for reading and best wishes on your path to success and independence as a young adult.

BIBLIOGRAPHY

- *Best Budgeting Apps for Teens (I Tried Them All)* https://www.kidsmoney. org/teens/budgeting/apps/
- *Can a Teenager Have a Bank Account? | Chase* https://www.chase.com/ personal/banking/education/basics/can-a-teenager-open-a-bank-account#:~:text=How%20a%20teenager%20-can%20open,your%20bank%20for%20what's%20required.
- *Credit Scores 101: A Beginner's Guide For Teens and Young ...* https:// piscataqua.com/2024/02/14/credit-scores-101-a-beginners-guide-for-teens-and-young-adults/#:~:text=A%20credit%20score%20is%20al-most,trustworthy%20you%20appear%20to%20lenders.
- *How to file your federal income tax return* https://www.usa.gov/file-taxes
- *10 Essential Kitchen Tools for Beginner Cooks - Bon Appetit* https://www. bonappetit.com/story/10-essential-kitchen-tools-beginner-cooks
- *Twenty kitchen skills every teen needs to know before they ...* https://www. organiccookeryschool.org/blog//20-kitchen-skills-every-teen-needs-to-know-before-they-leave-for-uni
- *How to Understand and Use the Nutrition Facts Label* https://www.fda. gov/food/nutrition-facts-label/how-understand-and-use-nutrition-facts-label
- *Meal Planning For Beginners (Meal Plan Template Inside!)* https:// workweeklunch.com/meal-planning-for-beginners/
- *SMART Goals and Your Teen* https://theblueheartfoundation.org/smart-goals-and-your-teen/
- *The Eisenhower Matrix: How to prioritize your to-do list* https://asana. com/resources/eisenhower-matrix
- *The Pomodoro Technique — Why it works & how to do it* https://todoist. com/productivity-methods/pomodoro-technique
- *Teenage Time Management Apps: 5 Best Picks for Focus* https:// teencoachacademy.com/blog/teenage-time-management-apps/
- *Hygiene: pre-teens and teenagers* https://raisingchildren.net.au/pre-teens/healthy-lifestyle/hygiene-dental-care/hygiene-pre-teens-teens

- *Best teen skin care routine, according to dermatologists* https://www.cnn.com/cnn-underscored/beauty/teen-skin-care-routine
- *Types of Hair: How to Style and Care for Your Hair Type* https://www.healthline.com/health/beauty-skin-care/types-of-hair
- *Attire Guide: Dress Codes from Casual to White Tie* https://emilypost.com/advice/attire-guide-dress-codes-from-casual-to-white-tie
- *Learn How to Perform First Aid* https://www.redcross.org/take-a-class/first-aid
- *Make A Plan* https://www.ready.gov/plan
- *Home Natural Gas Safety Tips & Leak Symptoms | Constellation* https://www.constellation.com/energy-101/home-natural-gas-safety-tips.html
- *Earthquakes* https://www.ready.gov/earthquakes
- *10 Signs Your Teen Is Stressed Out* https://www.verywellmind.com/signs-your-teen-is-stressed-out-2611336
- *How to Use Mindfulness Therapy for Anxiety: 15 Exercises* https://positivepsychology.com/mindfulness-for-anxiety/
- *Resilience in pre-teens & teenagers* https://raisingchildren.net.au/pre-teens/development/social-emotional-development/resilience-in-teens
- *Kids, Teens and Young Adults* https://www.nami.org/your-journey/kids-teens-and-young-adults/
- *Tips for Teens: Building Healthy Communication Skills* https://www.thrivetrainingconsulting.com/tips-for-teens-building-healthy-communication-skills/
- *How to Practice Active Listening: 16 Examples & Techniques* https://positivepsychology.com/active-listening-techniques/
- *25 Tips to Help Your Teen Make Friends: It Doesn't Have ...* https://raisingteenstoday.com/tips-to-help-your-teen-make-friends/
- *Conflict management with pre-teens and teenagers* https://raisingchildren.net.au/teens/communicating-relationships/communicating/conflict-management-with-teens
- *ONET® Career Exploration Tools** https://www.onetcenter.org/tools.html
- *Resume Examples for Teens: Template and Writing Tips* https://www.indeed.com/career-advice/resumes-cover-letters/resume-examples-for-teens

- *Tips for Young Adults Going On Their First Job Interview* https://foundationsasheville.com/tips-for-young-adults-going-on-their-first-job-interview/
- *Top 12 benefits of networking: Why networking is important* https://www.michaelpage.com.au/advice/career-advice/career-progression/top-12-benefits-networking-why-networking-important
- *Plumbing 101: The Ultimate Beginner's Guide* https://plumbingconcepts.com/plumbing-101-the-ultimate-beginners-guide/
- *Electrical safety lessons for teens* https://www.kentuckyliving.com/energy/electrical-safety-lessons-for-teens
- *Appliance Care and Maintenance Tips to Make ...* https://www.familyhandyman.com/list/appliance-care-and-maintenance-tips-to-make-appliances-last/
- *A Whole-House Cleaning Schedule You'll Actually Stick To* https://www.bhg.com/homekeeping/house-cleaning/tips/whole-house-cleaning-schedule/
- *What Every Teen Needs to Know About Their Digital ...* https://www.netnanny.com/blog/what-every-teen-needs-to-know-about-their-digital-footprint/
- *25 Essential Data Privacy Best Practices in 2023* https://www.enzuzo.com/blog/data-privacy-best-practices
- *10 Common Scams Targeted at Teens* https://www.investopedia.com/financial-edge/1012/common-scams-targeted-at-teens.aspx
- *Teens and social media use: What's the impact?* https://www.mayoclinic.org/healthy-lifestyle/tween-and-teen-health/in-depth/teens-and-social-media-use/art-20474437
- *Money-Saving Apps for Teens: Budgeting, Tracking, and ...* https://www.azcentralcu.org/blog/money-saving-apps-for-teens/
- *Public Transportation Safety Tips* https://www.springfieldmo.gov/307/Public-Transportation-Safety-Tips
- *How to Read a Lease* https://www.investopedia.com/articles/personal-finance/090315/millennials-guide-how-read-lease.asp
- *Car Maintenance Basics Everyone Should Know* https://www.familyhandyman.com/list/car-maintenance-basics-everyone-should-know/
- *The Importance of Goal-Setting for Teens* https://www.bgca.org/news-stories/2022/January/the-importance-of-goal-setting-for-teens/

- *Journaling for Personal Growth: The Impact of ...* https://www.rosebud. app/blog/journaling-for-personal-growth
- *Carol Dweck: A Summary of Growth and Fixed Mindsets* https://fs.blog/ carol-dweck-mindset/
- *30 Gratitude Activities for Kids and Teens* https://www. thepathway2success.com/30-gratitude-activities-for-kids-and-teens/

www.ingramcontent.com/pod-product-compliance
Lightning Source LLC
Chambersburg PA
CBHW020357130626
46549CB00006B/2324